Successful Project Management

Successful
Project Management

W. J. TAYLOR · T. F. WATLING

Business Books Limited · London

First published 1970

WILLIAM JOHN TAYLOR   THOMAS FRANCIS WATLING

ISBN 0 220 99261 4

This book has been set in 10 on 12 pt Times
printed in England by C. Tinling & Co. Ltd, Prescot Lancs.
for the publishers, Business Books Limited
(registered office: 180 Fleet Street, London, E.C.4),
publishing offices: Mercury House, Waterloo Road, London, S.E.1.

MADE AND PRINTED IN GREAT BRITAIN

Acknowledgements

In writing this book we have been greatly helped by the friendly criticism of our colleagues Mr N. D. Hill and Mr J. R. Cartwright. We are also grateful to our colleague Mr D. W. Pygott for the helpful provision of library services.

The typing of the manuscript, a laborious task, was cheerfully undertaken by Miss Chris Weston and Miss Carole Duggan, to whom we are indebted.

Last but not least we are more than conscious of the forbearance of our wives.

Contents

part two The Essential Steps

part four Project Choice

part five Further Project Considerations

List of illustrations

part one Why Project Management?

one What is Project Management?

Are you a Project Manager?

Do you want to be one?

Perhaps you are already one without knowing it?

A good many people are involved in project management without knowing it. They can improve their performance by studying and applying the techniques of project management. The surveyor designing and producing maps of virgin territory and the site agent in charge of a small building site are Project Managers just as surely as those who carry the title. Here are some examples of people who could use project management techniques to great advantage to themselves and their companies as they are performing some form of project management.

Engineering Industries

Production Engineers and
   Supervisors
Project Engineers
Project Managers
Works Managers

Production Managers
Manufacturing Services
   Managers
Project Leaders
Administration Officer and
   Managers

General Businesses, Local and National Government

Administration and Services	Town Planners
Officers and Managers	Town Executives
Computer Managers	Business Owners
Office Managers	

Building and Civil Engineering Industries

Site Agents	Project Managers
Contract Managers	Planning Staff
Clerk of Works	General Management
Quantity Surveyors	

Who are Project Managers?

Let's look at descriptions of Project Managers, or people doing project management work, written in some advertisements by consultant organizations and companies. The diversity of the meaning of the term 'Project Manager' or other title describing a form of project management can be readily seen.

The trades, professions and examples listed show then that project management is a wide subject and can be applied by many people to many jobs, but there are reasons for talking about project management rather than just 'management'.

We shall discuss in later chapters the role of line or functionally orientated management and the need for lateral or 'across function lines' co-ordination. When the task or job reaches such proportions of size, complexity or other definition that additional management is organized in lateral co-ordination, this management is usually termed project management. Its function is to drive the project forward as a project; line management by definition must concern itself primarily with its line function tasks. What is the role of the Project Manager in these cases? In the fullest sense the Project Manager must:

Prepare and progress the overall project plan in terms of cost, time and function.

Be the central authority for technical and management decisions on the project.

Be responsible for the successful conclusion of the project in terms of cost, time and function.

Have equal influence with the line managers in order to plan the use and allocation of resources.

Be the reporting authority to higher management for the project.

Some companies are built around a series of large projects. Examples are mining finance houses, atomic power companies, oil production companies and construction companies. In recent years, project management techniques have been used to an increasing extent in advanced technological manufacturing industry.

Project management is two things: a management arrangement and a system of management techniques. Why the management arrangement? We can see in Fig. 1.1 that even with a few function lines, in this example 4, the co-ordination routes possible, and nearly always necessary, are $n \times (n-1) = 12$ in this case. Value n is equal to the number of interrelating organizations, divisions, sections, etc. With this sort of quantity the line managers would probably have little difficulty in providing co-ordination.

In Fig. 1.2 the number of functional lines necessary has grown and there is confusion of many function lines requiring inordinate amounts of line management work to get any project result at all. There is no effective result towards interfunctional goals. There is likely to be lateness and high costs, together with a lack of success of operation.

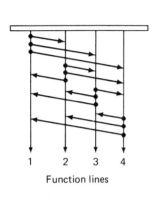

Function lines

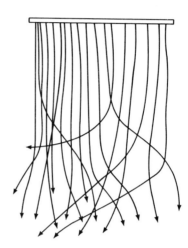

Fig. 1.1 Simple co-ordination routes   Fig. 1.2 Many function lines

The great danger is that people farthest down the management chain have no conception of the co-ordination required and those further up the chain may realize it, but be too busy with line function work to achieve it. With a project management arrangement there is a control on the multi-threads of vertical, functional management, from a project viewpoint as well as a technical skills area viewpoint. Two illustrations giving pictorial analogies to this control are Figs. 1.3 and 1.4.

Whether or not the full organization and responsibilities of project management are effected in a company, the techniques that have grown up rapidly with project management can always be applied. In our opinion these techniques ensure a practical approach to management, strip some of the mystery away from descriptions of management theory and philosophy and give a firm base for advancement to higher grades of management.

7

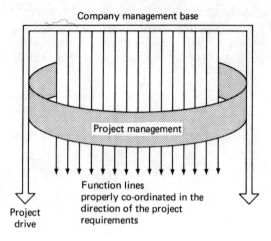

Fig. 1.3 Project management band analogy

Cylinder analogy

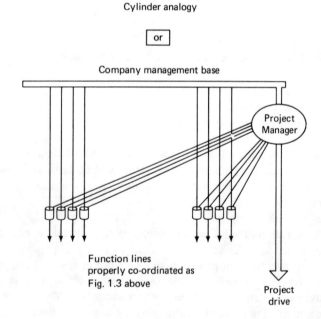

Fig. 1.4 Project management function line guides

Vital Factors in Management

In the management of all businesses, crafts, professions, even government service, small and large projects and small and large companies, there are three vital factors to bring success to an enterprise.

> Basic entrepreneurial ability, i.e. invention or innovation and selling ability.
> Treatment of people.
> Knowledge of management techniques.

Item 1, the basic entrepreneurial ability, can be taught, but more often than not it is an innate sense; it includes a complete awareness of situations and the apparent ability to make more right decisions than wrong ones. It is equally true to say that management techniques, item 3, are always called upon even unconsciously by the best entrepreneurs. They are only too well aware of the difficulty, and in many cases, impossibility of making correct decisions based upon their basic entrepreneurial abilities alone.

The treatment of people, item 2, has always been important but is increasingly recognized as such in this age when people are becoming more and more aware of the possibilities of life, both from pure materialistic and job satisfaction points of view. The subject can be taught, but once again an intrinsic desire to understand people is an essential part of success in this field.

With regard to item 3, the knowledge of management techniques; these definitely can be taught, and this is what we set out to do in this book. Without this knowledge people of good intelligence, having entrepreneurial ability and a desire to know, understand and manage people may well fail in their own businesses. To those of us who are employed to use our talents for someone else, it is even more important to know these techniques. It is the main weapon in our armoury to ensure that we can find the time to keep abreast of our various subjects and thus be competitive in our jobs. Not only this, most of us wish to advance, and without a secure base of successful techniques we shall be too busy with our hourly problems to have time to think. Thinking is essential to plan success; management techniques give you time to think.

9

The Key Techniques

In examining project management techniques it is necessary to identify the key items that comprise a successful project. The need for this definition was recognized during and immediately after the Second World War, especially in the United States but also in Great Britain. The war, with its accent on science, complex projects (especially the aircraft industry), urgency of completions and vital need for success, forced a new look at management techniques. Intuitive management cannot stand up to the pressure of increasingly complex situations: discipline of operation and the aid of more tools, such as computers, must be the aim of the modern manager in all grades of management.

The definition of the key techniques in project management stems from a very simple beginning; the strict logical examination of the way virtually any task in the business world is performed.

We ask the following questions about the task. We carry out the key techniques!

**Key technique 1
Define the task**

What is the task?

Describe it. Identify it.

Specify it in as much detail as possible.

Make sure everybody who has to assist in the definition does so.

To define a task we must ask questions and receive answers that fit the other answers. We may have to innovate in some areas; other areas may not yet be fully clear. Definition never really ceases, but we have to be complete enough to enable the next committal of resources to occur with the minimum risk that we can arrange — By Definition.
Definition includes:

The general overall system and requirements.

What are we really trying to do or to make?

What are the principal functions?

What special features exist?

What new research, design, engineering or manufacturing processes or techniques are there?

What special other demands are there on the company or its subcontractors?

Are there new standards of quality or reliability, packing, deliveries, quantities?

Are there special timescales, prices, costs, penalties, risks?

Eventually, we must be able to DEFINE THE TASK such that we have full confidence that all the known facts and points that we should anticipate because of the company expertise are combined to specify THE DEFINED TASK.

A LAST WORD

With all the care in the world, definitions do change. Be prepared for change: technology changes, priority changes, requirements change, business changes.

Fig. 1.5 Key technique 1

Key technique 2
Know what total resources are required
to perform the task

In terms of finance.

In human effort, physical and mental.

In materials and equipment.

In space to perform the task.

In services to enable the task to be performed.

There are further breakdowns of these:

Finance implies provision, budgets, cash flow and risk analysis.

Human effort must be defined in terms of type, grade, ability and suitability. It also refers to supervision and management types and ability.

Materials include special raw materials, plant, equipment and consumable items.

Space includes land, buildings and room therein.

Services extend from such facilities as a convenient port for shipping to electrical and gas supply.

Remember that inherent in the decisions made about resources must be the realization of the effects upon timescales, quality, reliability, costs and product cost.

A LAST WORD

Spare resources of all types are nearly always required. Unforeseen problems have a habit of occurring regularly.

Fig. 1.6 Key technique 2

Key technique 3
Know the timescale in terms of all activities,
events and resources

To obtain the resources.

To apply and employ the resources.

If the timescale is already specified then the resources have to meet it if this is feasible and economically viable.

If the timescale is not already specified the resources must be chosen to meet an acceptable, as well as an economical and viable, timetable.

While bearing in mind the above, the earlier a project is completed the greater its marketability power. (This applies to projects which are not pre-ordered small quantity lines.)

Shorter timescales without accompanying 'crash' costs enabling earlier sales give better cash flow returns on the investment.

In the building up of a complete time plan for a project a considerable number of activities will normally emerge. Some of the logic will be fixed, but it will be advantageous to thoroughly examine the logic as well as activity times.

A LAST WORD

Humans, contrary to some popular opinions, are normally optimistic! Bear this in mind when assessing critical timescales!

Fig. 1.7 Key technique 3

Key technique 4
What quality and reliability have to be
achieved?

They may be already specified, in which case the resources and timescale have to be suitably adjusted.

If they are not already specified a decision must be made as to what standards the quality and reliability shall be.

There are always repercussions on other key items in that:

Timescales will be affected.

Resources will change.

Costs and perhaps prices will have to change.

With modern technology and value control techniques, quality and reliability can be obtained at no extra cost, and in some cases at less cost.

Look for newer technologies.

Look for less parts.

Look for 'best' value. Use value analysis and engineering techniques.

A LAST WORD

Unless you are a 'get rich today and move on tonight' company (which we doubt) then quality and reliability must be acceptable to the customer at a market price he is prepared to pay. Quality and reliability are worth striving for.

Fig. 1.8 Key technique 4

Key technique 5
Know the product cost!

To know the product cost is vital, common sense we could say!
To know the product cost accurately is one of the greatest
strengths a company can have. If you really know the costs then
a lot of other activities are probably going right: purchasing,
estimating, process planning, production engineering, value
engineering, etc.

The price may be set by marketing only or other
considerations, or it may be set after establishment
of costs or both.

Price — Cost = Profit!

Notwithstanding the above, don't economize on
critical path items that are a small part of the
total cost or where the number of items make the
amortized increase of cost each a small percentage
of the original cost.

Watch quality, reliability and function when cost
reductions are being planned.

Until the product cost is known in absolute detail, part by part,
function by function and with the proper overheads by cost centres,
effective cost design is not possible. How can one way be thought
'better' than another and the cost not known? Designers need
costs as much as they need slide rules.

Learn to 'fill the pot' of product cost.
(See Chapter 7.)

Continually press the company organization for more
efficient, fast and accurate costing.

A LAST WORD

There are few products that are not rigidly controlled by the market place, i.e. *price*
is fixed by *competition*. Cost *and hence profits* are in *your* hands.

Fig. 1.9 Key technique 5

Key technique 6
Make a continuous, conscious, disciplined
approach to optimize the value

Value must always be in part intangible: beauty
in the eye of the beholder and all that; why we like
one object better than another; what are we getting
for our money.

There are, however, other aspects of the value question.
Tangible items!

Is the whole task successful?

Is the cost/time/quality/success of function
relationship in proper balance?

Value is optimum when the 'function' is obtained
at the lowest cost with an acceptable timescale and
quality.

Use value analysis.

Use value engineering.

Value optimization of a product also brings other benefits. There is
a build up of activity in all parts of the business to achieve maximum
value. This can extend to subcontractors and their subcontractors.

Get the best value from bought out materials and
finished goods, not by beating down your
subcontractors but by bringing them into your
value optimization schemes.

Let them be competitive, yes!

Let them make a profit, yes!

A LAST WORD

Profit is the motive for business. Value means profit for everybody, the customer
included. If the customer gets value, there is more business, more profit. Q.E.D!

Fig. 1.10 Key technique 6

Key technique 7
Measure project performance

Key technique 7 is simply repeating Key techniques 1 to 6 throughout the life of the project.
In so doing, the complete project performance is continually measured and the control over the project is deepened.

Like steering a car or a boat, an assessment is continually made of the position and corrections made.

We must try to identify problems in advance by our detailed knowledge, measurement and control of the project. We can then take corrective action.

After measurement comes assessment and controlling actions.

With measurement and control comes management information. Make sure top management is never in the dark about your project. Could you help your staff efficiently without knowledge of their problems?

Watch especially the top level key events or baselines (see Chapter 9). These are jumping off platforms to the next major activity. Don't fall into deep water!

Measure the performance of everything affecting the project: subcontractors, all company personnel who are contributing and customer contributions, e.g. premises, payments, etc.

A LAST WORD

Measurement and control take time and effort. Without them there may be no time. Your project is unlikely to survive.

Fig. 1.11 Key technique 7

Figure 1.12 gives us a picture of the project management process with the key techniques noted against the items.

Systems Approach

It becomes clear in examining the key techniques that there is little independence between them. For example, if the resources are

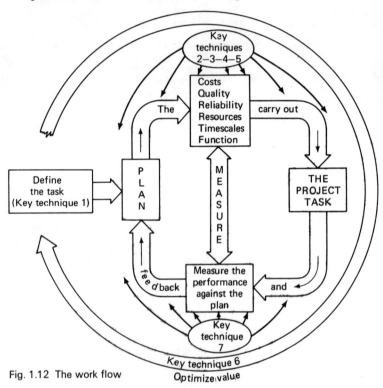

Fig. 1.12 The work flow

increased without high quality or an increased specification of the task then the value per unit falls. There may be an effect on the timescale as well.

This interdependence upon one another puts the key techniques into a unique position—they form a system of actions—one is not altered without knowing the effect on one or more of the others. This is what makes successful project management different from a naive, inexperienced or unenlightened approach.

Successful project management is an integrated systems approach to the project or task, an awareness of all the key techniques and their influence on one another. Much management just happens because of recurring crises; in a substantial number of cases this is because management is caught with no planned approach. To get out of this vicious circle requires effort on the part of the persons responsible, over and above the daily round, until the correct plans are laid to stop the crisis of 'tomorrow'. A lot of this book is devoted to practical planning for that very reason and all the techniques fit together to form a system; to take in its stride any crisis and put it where it belongs—in the 'dealt with' file—without throwing near panic into the proper supervision or management activities.

Progressing

The plan that will be derived if we use all the project management techniques detailed in this book will be a good one. It will stand up to all the tests that higher management, the Board of Directors, or colleagues can give it but, and this is so important that we introduce it at this stage, no plan can remain rigid forever. Plans have to change in the light of information feedback from the execution of those plans. It is therefore vital that the plan is progressed correctly, and only by this progressing can the feedback information be brought to light. After working hard on the plan we must be on guard against leaning back and saying 'that's a job well done'. The project will not run itself, however good the plan. Progress measurement in as much depth as possible must be carried out all the time to anticipate potential problems. Progressing takes time but it need only take a small percentage of the total when the groundwork of the project has been properly laid.

Is Project Management Easy?

No! But it can be made much easier by knowing, not only the particular technical skills that may be necessary in any industry, but the methods common to all project management. These methods are fully covered in the subsequent chapters—they are not difficult individually—and like physical exercises they require to be practised regularly. They will rapidly become part of the subconscious actions of the user with the consequent improvement in individual job efficiency and the success it will bring. The ultimate success for the company and the individuals is when the techniques are used in the organizational setting in which they were originally developed.

two The Need for Project Management and the Benefits

SO FAR WE HAVE been stressing a need for a system of key techniques to perform the task of project management. It is a fact, of course, that project management and project management techniques are separable in that project management techniques can be carried out in any situation of management even though a project management system as such is not being operated. This chapter deals more with the benefits of the system of project management than with the techniques themselves.

Benefits to the Company or Organization

In talking to managers in many companies, it becomes clear that companies are by no means united in thought on project management; only some have definite attitudes on the subject. There are those who say that they cannot see the need for project management; they have a functionally orientated management, perfectly capable of dealing with the work they have and they require no central interface for any of their jobs. Indeed, they do not class the jobs as projects at all, but simply as one kind of output or another. It is obvious in other companies that project management has been at work for a number of years and that company and individuals are well used to the system, picking up various projects and carrying them to fruition, building up and suspending staff and picking up other projects. This is, of course, especially true in the civil engineering industry, where contract managers might be building a bridge one year and some other type of work another year, with labour picked up as necessary from within the company and outside.

Other companies are playing with project management; they have some idea of the possible benefits, but are used to working with a functionally orientated system and are slow to adapt.

In pursuing the above statements, one must be careful not to be dogmatic in the cause of project management to the extent of saying that all companies should have project management. In the case of mass production products where there is no conjunction of these at later stages into more complex, more customer participation products, product management in organization terms may be of no advantage. However, all companies benefit from the use of project management techniques, even if they believe they cannot operate a complete system. Companies that benefit most are those where the various skills of the company have to be brought closely together to carry out a task of a specialist or complex character and often where a large amount of technological advance is being made. The field is wide and includes such items as:

Airfields	A computer system
A new business	Buildings projects
A missile system	A consortium project
Complete factories	Iron/steel complexes
Housing estates	Flood control systems
Bridges	Signalling systems
Process control installation	A new printing machine
Printed circuit production	Maintenance projects
Mining projects	Overseas aid projects
Ships	Power stations
Oil refineries	Railway signalling and control
Aeroplanes	Roads
Railways	Any technologically advanced
You have a go!	system
	Hundreds and thousands of others!

These projects all require a high degree of co-ordination, some much deeper than others. They will certainly involve many organizations within the company and outside contractors. The inter-organization involvement and cross co-ordination cannot be provided by only the long term planning down each functional 'leg' of the company. They demand a common technical and managerial interface and thus one person to look after them—a Project Manager.

To see how such a system can operate and then to weigh the benefits, we should look at the way many companies are built in terms of organization and functional groups, and how project management comes into the picture.

Organizations and Functional Groups

Organizations are groups of people and facilities set up within a company to perform single or multiple tasks. An organization can be a company or several organizations can comprise a company. In general, the need to divide the company into organizations (groups, divisions and sections are also other words used to describe this compartment forming process) arises from a desire to:

Put like operations in one compartment.

Keep unlike operations apart.

This applies, for example, to:

Sales.

Research and development.

Production.

Commercial and accounting.

The advantages of this arrangement are several:

Budgeting and control is easier as skill is attained in a particular group or organization.

The particular overall technical skills of the organization can be fostered because of the narrower field.

Responsibility for that part of the company is more easily defined.

There will be 'division of labour' advantages in some areas.

The disadvantage is the normal one of functionally orientated organizations, that overall co-ordination can really only be vested in the Managing Director. This is correct for those aspects of the business a Managing Director should attend to, but immediately below him there is no one in authority to deal *effectively and rapidly* with *project* problems. There is a need for cross functional co-ordination. The simple structure of many companies appears in Fig. 2.1.

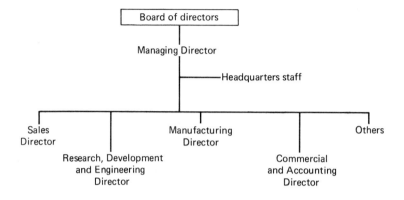

Fig. 2.1 Simple company structure

The usual remedy for project problems is the setting up of committees to deal with them. Let us not echo the usual universal condemnation of committees; they can be made to work and very effectively, but in many cases they are ineffective simply because the members are not fully aware of their authority or real function and, sadly, individual members are often biased in favour of protecting their own line management organization.

The result too often is as portrayed by Fig. 1.2 in Chapter 1— Confusion! Still retaining a fairly simple approach there is a further breakdown, namely functional within product, employed in some large companies where the Fig. 2.1 layout would apply to a single or related group of products as shown in Fig. 2.2.

Groups A, C and D would be subdivided as shown for Group B. The Headquarters staff with functional specialization, e.g. Chief Engineer, Chief Accountant, etc. would have functional links to the respective Group Managers.

The added advantage in this structure over that in Fig. 2.1 are:

A profit consciousness can be more easily engendered in the product group as it can be operated in a similar way to a separate company.

23

Profitable product groups can be fostered and unprofitable ones cut out as the recognition of each is easier.

Lateral co-ordination within a product group will be easier as the unit is decreased in size.

Morale is likely to be better because of the personal association with the end product.

The added disadvantages are:

Specialist activities, e.g. sales, accounting, etc. are now split into the product groups and will require co-ordination at the company headquarters level.

Multi-product systems, i.e. a system sold by the company incorporating several product group products will require extra co-ordination.

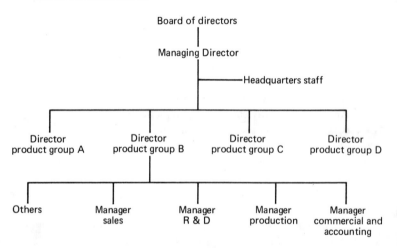

Fig. 2.2 Product groups

The interesting point about this type of management, and indeed physical structure, is that as the number of products within these product groups gets smaller, the product group looks more and more like a project management organization where the product Group Director is the Project Manager. This is especially so where these product groups are in different locations and cannot enjoy common services.

Lateral or Project Co-ordination

Under the Directorates or Management so far illustrated, there will be a management hierarchy and, in fact, it may consist of several layers of management, e.g. under the Sales Director there could be Regional Managers (perhaps some regions being overseas); under the Regional Managers, District Managers; under these Area Managers; and finally numbers of senior and junior salesmen.

Consider what happens if the company offers to supply an integrated system comprising items from all product groups in Fig. 2.2, bearing in mind the management hierarchy. The company must take an overall look at:

The system needs and costs.
The equipment requirements and costs.
The equipment availability.
The tender to the customer.
The subsequent implementation.

There are several ways in which this work might be carried out:

One part of one of the groups could be asked to co-ordinate the others likely to be involved.

This would probably be the group having the largest part of the system to develop.

Staff from headquarters could be asked to co-ordinate the activities.
Other person(s) within the company could be called upon.
A Project Manager could be appointed to 'manage' the project.

Unless the latter is done, the result is certain to be a poor second choice of method, with also the certainty that senior executives are increasingly going to be loaded with *project* co-ordination problems in addition to their normal line functions.

If the project is complex; organizationally, technically or financially large then a central technical and managerial interface must be created, i.e. a project management organization and a Project Manager. Without this the project will invariably be late, much more costly and perhaps with inferior function. A project needs nurture and drive as a project and the application of all project management key techniques.

25

As we saw in Chapter 1, the number of co-ordination routes in a simple organization with only 4 function line ends to co-ordinate is 12. With a more typical figure of, say, 30 in a small project, the routes number 870.

Compare this with the immediate advantage of a project system. In theory there are now only 30 routes; in practice, of course, there will have to be some inter-organization co-ordination at various levels in addition to the minimum quantity. If the quantity reached 100, the gain in route complexity would be nearly 900 per cent. This, however, is only the start of the advantage.

There is a project pulse now beating from the central heart; the project impetus grows all the time and all participants become project conscious—it's their project! Personnel problems become easier because when people have a common goal, or common enemy, they fight together, not each other.

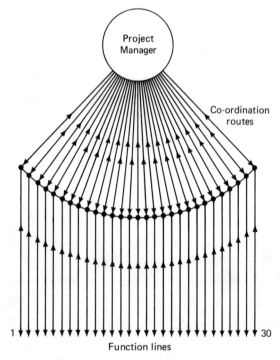

Fig. 2.3 Project co-ordination routes

A simple example of the interaction of project parts at various stages of their life cycle and the need for project management of one type or another is the construction of, say, a large block of flats. In the offices of the main contractor preliminary work is carried out on drawings, plans, costs, specifications and appropriate timescales in order that the various planning permissions can be obtained. When it is clear that the project can proceed, detailed plans of all activities must be made, dovetailing the activities of all types of skills to ensure that the project finishes on time and at the correct cost.

It will be assumed that several subcontractors are engaged, apart from the main contractor, on items such as:

Precast concrete units.
Steel construction.
Heating and ventilating.
Electrical.
Flooring.
Plastering.
Glazing.

The subcontract orders and timing together with the ordering of all materials to arrive at planned times must be achieved. Whatever initial success there might be in planning will be lost if materials are not on site at the right time.

When the project commences, the site can be cleared and foundation concrete or pile driving commenced. Even at this early stage and with this seemingly single task there are many complications that will arise that will demand someone on site to judge and take appropriate action.

The site clearance.

Has it started? Is it going to be ready for the excavators? If not, what action must be taken?

When the site is cleared and foundation digging or pile driving commenced.

Is the machinery there?

Are the plans understood?

What action has to be taken about the drains that no one knew were there?

Are all the materials, machinery and men ready for concrete mixing as fast as the diggings are completed?

When the foundations are complete.

Are the precast concrete units on site?

Are the steel workers and steel available for the first steel work?

Now all these items with good planning will take place in some way, but because the chance of (n) items all being 100 per cent effective is below unity, there are inevitably many actions and decisions, daily, to take on site to ensure an adequate and instantaneous correction of deficiencies. It is rare to vest these actions equally between several people, as the interaction of decisions is not likely to provide the best answer to the problems. There is normally a site agent who is responsible to see the job proceeds smoothly. He may delegate to assistants, but overall there is one view, his view, of the position on site, and the consequent corrective and advisory functions.

When the structure is sufficiently complete, the heating and ventilating engineers, the electricians and glaziers, will be instructed to start work. There will be problems. Holes will not have been left in concrete where they should have been; additional electrical points may be necessary; rework may have to be done after inspection, and subcontractors may have to be firmly handled. There must be a constant drive by the site agent to ensure:

> That all tasks, however small, are completed on time without extra cost to his company.
>
> That the plans laid down for the construction are adhered to, unless they are patently wrong.
>
> That the quality of the work is consistent with the company, local government and central government criteria.
>
> That actions are taken throughout the job which will enable the completion to be achieved on time, at the planned cost with proper regard to safety and wellbeing of all workers.

The job was a block of flats. The man in charge was called a Site Agent. He was a Project Manager.

Difficulties of Project Management

There are three main areas of difficulty in project management. Two concern the work content itself: the technical difficulties overall, and the external factors continually influencing the position, such as component deliveries or subcontract labour. The third area, however, can often be the most difficult; the attitude of management at various levels towards the Project Manager and, indeed, the idea of project management having to exist at all. It is generally acknowledged and seen to be so in a large section of various types of industry that the functionally orientated structure is superior in, say, the design, production engineering, manufacture, etc. areas in the sense that each skill is applied more effectively when measured as a skill alone. The managers of these skills are quite rightly jealous of them and often resent any attempt at co-ordination across these 'skill barriers'. The resentment is usually manifest in a lack of co-operation with the Project Manager or his staff. It is indeed unfortunate that this can be so, and reflects the general lack of appreciation of the weaknesses in all vertically structured, functionally orientated managements. A typical example of this can be the case of a design passing into manufacture. The design engineers should work closely with production engineers to ensure that the design is fit for production. The production engineers may be responsible to the factory manager, or they may be on a staff basis and answerable to neither the Head of Design nor manufacture. In any event, this interface of design through production to manufacture can be a difficult one. Because the designers and production engineers are often answerable to different management lines, decisions can be taken based upon differing views, e.g. designers are often in a hurry, development timescales are tight; production engineering can be insufficient, quantities can be ill defined so that uneconomic methods of manufacture occur and costs rise. It is here that a Project Manager can, and certainly has to, exercise firm diplomacy and technical skill to ensure a smooth passage of the design into production. In many organizations, some of the production engineers become project engineers, and carry out the role of Project Manager in this limited, but important area of the total job.

To sum up, an important difficulty of application of project management is the non-acceptance by the line management of the company, who believe the labour division by skills and their own infallibility, will be sufficient. It is only when the big, awkward or complex job comes along that the company suddenly discovers the tremendous co-ordination effort required below the Managing Director or top executive level, and forthwith pins the responsibility on the head of its favourite manager. It is a fact, of course, that mediocre project management may be better than none at all, so that the job looks like a success. It would, however, be much better to realize in advance the advantages, and choose the project management structure and managers other than at a crisis time. It also seems a foregone conclusion that as the technological complexity grows so project management will become more and more necessary.

Benefits to the Individual

You do not have to be a Project Manager or your company to have project management organizations before you can receive the benefits from knowing the techniques of project management. There are many people who, like you, will be skilled in a particular trade or profession, either working alone, with others or in management. All these people are communicating with others in their company or business, field of business or with other companies.

You will have seen in Chapter 1 that three vital factors were illustrated for successful management of all businesses, crafts, professions, etc. One was a basic entrepreneurial ability, another was treatment of people and the third was management techniques. You will have also seen in Chapter 1 that method and practice is the way in which management techniques can become automatic. If you follow and always carry out these key techniques, the really important top information in any project will be driven out of its hiding place and come to hand. The project management system of asking questions, planning jobs and arranging the work reveals the important points which stand alone from the unimportant, and gives a superior knowledge to the person who is following these techniques.

As an individual then you will, by learning how to operate project management techniques, be in possession of greater knowledge and hence greater power. We hope that by the time you have read this book, the benefits to the individual who pursues the successful project management techniques will become very clear indeed.

If your company operates a project management system, a period of time in a project management team or as a Project Manager can often be a fast lane to promotion because of the central and significant position that the project management team is likely to occupy. In view of the increasing complexity of industry generally, project management will be required in more and more companies. An adequate preparation to meet the challenge of this work is essential. It is also true to say that in many cases, age is not a barrier. There is room for all who know their business!

Benefits to the Customer

More and more as projects become larger, more costly and more complex the relationship between supplier and customer tends to get more complicated. It becomes essential that the supplier and the customer appoint one interface contact each, i.e. a Project Manager each. This does not prevent any extra contacts that may be necessary as the work proceeds, but does ensure that responsibility is sited in a single channel. Neither party has that great difficulty of knowing who to ask about a particular problem and decisions can be made much more quickly.

The customer feels he is being attended, not by a large inorganic mass that he cannot seem to penetrate, but by a real personal contact; he also feels that this contact is able to attend properly to *his* problem because of the ability of the Project Manager to access any required part of his company directly. You may consider this latter ability results in slight anarchy in terms of functional organizations, but it can and does work highly successfully and customers, once they have tasted the benefits, insist on a Project Manager.

Perhaps you have tried to contact, without much success, the right person to answer your query in a company. We are sure that people often get thoroughly exasperated during the process because they cannot seem to get a satisfactory interface with the company. Now consider a customer involved in a highly complicated link with your company. The customer cannot be allowed to get exasperated; you need him again!

three Choice of Project Manager and Structure of Project Management

Introduction

Like all management structures, there is no perfect solution and the final picture very much depends on what authority and real responsibility the Project Manager is to have. It certainly seems that the structure most likely to succeed is where project management operates in a high level co-ordinating role and with the minimum of direct staff. Extra staffing is achieved by secondment from line organizations. Direction of the project is achieved by the ability and character of the Project Manager allowing him to be respected and receive co-operation by all line management and staff. In addition, he should have a clear place in the company management.

It is often the case therefore that the Project Manager is more noted for his management technique expertise, his ability to 'get things done' and his ability to 'get on with people' than for his sheer technical prowess. However, it can be dangerous to minimize this latter talent when choosing Project Managers dependent upon the project type and size. The Project Manager should preferably be an expert either in the field of the project task or a subject allied to it. However, it must be acknowledged that in some types of project management 'non-technical' Project Managers may be successfully employed. Instead, the Project Manager may be a professional in a non-related sphere, e.g. accountant or company secretary.

Responsibilities of a Project Manager

Before the choice of a Project Manager is made, the task must be defined to determine who would be suitable to perform it.

Project management can occur, for example, in a very local sense in an electronics laboratory where a Project Manager is appointed to lead and effect the successful conclusion of a new design of electronic circuit, or control panel or computer input/output device. There is little doubt that full emphasis must be on technical knowledge of the particular subject, but all the key techniques must be applied. A very good design is useless if it is too late and costs too much in terms of unit cost, development or manufacture.

Project management may be concerned in any of the tasks of different natures that have been listed in Chapter 2, and all will demand a particular type of Project Manager.

Is the project to be controlled completely by the Project Manager, including all personnel and budgets? Even though a project is large, with much money at stake and many people involved, there is not a rigid rule as to whether the Project Manager should have executive responsibility in a line management sense and control the budget, or be a high level co-ordinator. Both systems, and arrangements between, operate successfully throughout industry.

How much money is at stake to be managed or co-ordinated by the Project Manager?

How many people will be directly under the Project Manager's control?

One of the most important responsibilities, however, of a Project Manager is to ensure that all parties from their respective functional operation or subcontract basis have a clear, unambiguous and common understanding of the project, its aims and complete purpose. This facet apart from any other is always instrumental in ensuring the highest chance of a successful project for the company.

Size of Project

If we draw a graph of 'size' of project against intimate allied technical knowledge of the Project Manager we are likely to arrive at something similar to Fig. 3.1. There would undoubtedly be argument on the percentages attributed to this or that facet of the task, and this or that ability of the Project Manager.

However, if 'size' means complexity, cost, number of organizations, subcontractors and skills involved, then Fig. 3.1 gives a fair representation of those projects having a large technical base, simply because it ultimately become impossible for one man to know it all. Other projects, e.g. overseas aid projects or those with a smaller direct technical base are nearer to the 'head of business' idea, because man management and project techniques, together with entrepreneurial abilities are required, much more than any particular intimate allied technical knowledge.

One of the items within the general term 'complexity' is the number of activity types that have to be brought into relationship

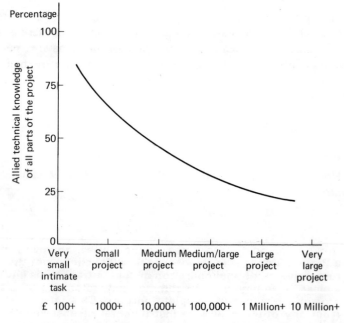

Fig. 3.1 Size of project vs. intimate technical knowledge

with one another. While the cost of a project may be high, say several millions (category 'large' in Fig. 3.1), the number of activity types may be small, compared with the total outlay.

This is a question of 'packages' of work and what influence the Project Manager can have over these 'packages'. It is quite conceivable that a project of 'smaller size' may be very complex in respect of the number of 'packages'. For example, a project worth £2 million may have 10 packages of work; a project worth £1 million may have 100 packages and be much harder to manage.

Technical Knowledge

While intimate technical knowledge of a major amount of the project is always desirable, it is essential that one part at least is known in some depth—in other words a technical slant on the project.

The Project Manager must be a professional in at least one subject. He is then likely to possess the basic disciplines which enable him to appreciate the problems of the project; to have the necessary humility to realize that expert advice and assistance must be sought at all times.

The key techniques must be interpreted in the light of the technical practice of the type of project. The peculiarities of specifications, site tests, customer practice, budgeting, etc. must be woven into the key techniques.

There are thousands of different types or shades of projects—each will dictate its own amount of technical ability required coupled with other abilities.

Personality

Except on the highly technical, intimate and small projects, he must be capable of managing others. In any case he must be able to organize, direct and control his own particular project. As the project size increases, he has to achieve this through other managers. His leadership must be forceful, but not ruthless; many people in the other organizations apart from his own must feel this force and be led to action for the project good. Invariably, there will be reaction problems for the Project Manager as his project drive will often be incompatible with the duties the line management staff are presently working on. The Project Manager will be aware of his ultimate authority on the major aspects of his project; he knows the company base management will back him; he is also aware that if he has to resort to this final authority time and time again, he is a failure as a Project Manager. All this sums up to tact and diplomacy and the ability to get work done without direct line authority over most of the staff involved.

Communication ability is a must for a Project Manager in all the normal methods and type of contact, i.e. personal, written or telephone contact by discussion, writing, speaking and negotiation. The significance of the communication is both internal and external. There will be very large amounts of internal communication from and to the Project Manager from many levels. This communication has to be successful in the main, otherwise the co-operation level will fall and the project suffers. Externally, it will be a certainty that the Project Manager will meet the customer as the central technical and management interface for his company. He must succeed in that communication of ideas and negotiations so that mutual trust and satisfaction are achieved.

In respect of creative requirements the Project Manager certainly must be able to create accurate and imaginative plans for the project, to anticipate more problems than overtake him. He must also be able to create or modify procedures and systems to suit the project. Technical design creation is not necessarily a priority, but it depends on the size and type of project.

The Project Manager must be able to take responsibility, because even in the non-executive or very normal situation of the Project Manager being a high level co-ordinator, he must be able to make decisions and control the destiny of the project. The responsibility will include the providing of advice which will generally be taken and thus influence the decisions of other people, i.e. line managers.

Knowing the Right People

INSIDE THE COMPANY

In the larger projects, it is undoubtedly necessary to either know the right people or know who are the right people because all the time the Project Manager has to seek assistance from people who can help him get work done. In any organization, notwithstanding the published charts of the management hierarchy and staff, there is always the unwritten organization that actually gets things done. There is nothing unusual about this; various people throughout the company will be of most use to the Project Manager notwithstanding that sometimes their apparent place in the hierarchy is not high nor well defined. It is not who the people are or what organization medals are on their chest that count; it is what they can perform that matters.

Now this is all very well to keep the project moving forward at high speed, but the Project Manager has still to get many approvals from the line managers, and this fact must be thoroughly acknowledged. The Project Manager must know the right people and who the right people are!

In this category of knowing people comes also the knowledge of the company structure, its rules and its procedures. Unless the Project Manager puts up a serious definite case to change the rules he should abide by them; not to do so is anarchy. There will be a great deal of temptation for this latter because rarely does line management work fast enough to keep pace with project requirements and there will be much frustration at times. Tact, charm, diplomacy, negotiation, some stubbonness, all will be necessary to win the day.

OUTSIDE THE COMPANY

Invariably, the larger the project the more the Project Manager is likely to meet, discuss and negotiate with the customer. In government and national industries projects, the knowledge of the right people is always necessary. This is not for the purpose that many people think, i.e. to influence decisions in a direct sense. What does occur is a greater understanding of the project problem as the customer sees it and to fit the project to that understanding. There may be two ways of meeting a specification, but one may be preferred even though both are of equal technical merit and cost.

Priority of Project

Project Managers may not readily admit it, but if the priority of the project is high enough then this affects some of the necessity for a 'better' Project Manager than on another project. Priority makes all the difference between a struggle by the Project Manager and a relatively easy job. A Project Manager always has two fights on his hands: one is the project and its problems as a project, the other is invariably the competition within his company of other projects struggling for attention. The temptation, however, to exchange priority for Project Manager prowess can be very dangerous— priorities change. The moral is clear. Choose the Project Manager for the job.

Structure of Project Management

Because the subject of management structures is so diverse and schemes which work well in one company are not suited in another, so the project management structure varies from company to company. It is not only the picture on the wall of the management structure that matters, it is the use of that picture that is more important. In many ways the picture of a conventional functional management system can be project management. Let us illustrate this; take a small company with, say, about 400 employees with a conventional management system as Fig. 3.2 below.

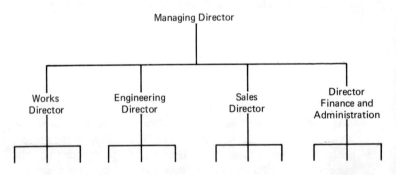

Fig. 3.2 Function line structure

If the company makes a product line in sufficient quantities to justify production runs of a single type multi-component article, then there would be no argument about it being a normal function-ally orientated company. Now take a similar company engaged in more complex products and in smaller quantity. Also assume that products are several in type and to some degree influenced by individual customer requirements. A need will now appear for more customer interaction through some responsibility thread inside the company, i.e. a lateral or product/project orientated approach. The general structure of the company still remains ostensibly as in Fig. 3.2. The lateral 'push' can be achieved in several ways as briefly mentioned in Chapter 2:

Project direction by one of the line managements: Fig. 3.3.
Staff function under the Managing Director: Fig. 3.4.
Programme or project management under the Managing Director and assuming project responsibility: Fig. 3.5.

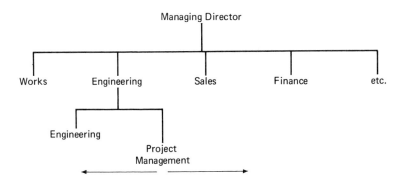

Fig. 3.3 Project management by a line function

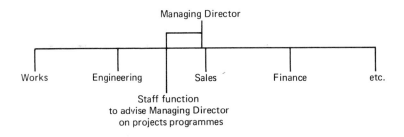

Fig. 3.4 Staff function to advise on progress

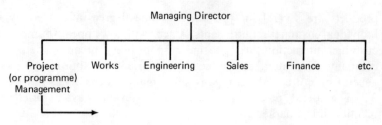

Fig. 3.5 Project (or program) separate management

Now take the idea of the complex products further. They are only a few types, have longer development timescales and are much more custom built. The organization structure then might become as it is set out in Fig. 3.6.

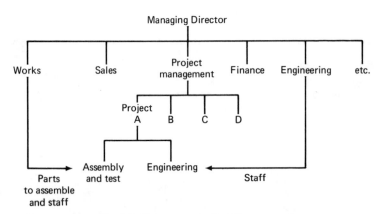

Fig. 3.6 Almost pure project management

There are some examples of this in several large companies, and in each case the remainder of the organization structure is as Fig. 2.2 with the Managing Director in Fig. 3.6 equivalent to the Product Group Director in Fig. 2.2.

Complete project orientated structures are comparatively rare and it appears that the best compromise is functional orientation, but with *acknowledged* project management and co-operation with it enforced by top management. Location can, of course, alter cases. If companies have several locations they may find that to all intents and purposes they operate pure project management, without calling it such, for at least part of their functional lines.

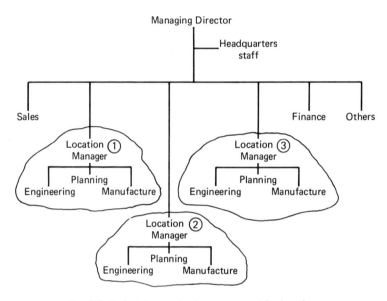

Fig. 3.7 Project (or product) management by location

If the products in location 1, 2 and 3 are specialized enough then the manager in each location is effectively the Project Manager, although not dealing with all function lines, e.g. sales.

Task Forces

Finally taking the case of a company with a few large projects, it may be more efficient to adapt specific teams to deal with them, i.e. split off a substantial part of the company into project forces while retaining the basic functional organization in other respects. Such an approach could well be suitable where a company was considering a traumatic change in its product range or a major new range of products.

41

four Defining the Project

WE HAVE SEEN THAT key technique 1 tells us to identify the task. How many simple illustrations can you think of where an identification of the task before the event would have been highly advantageous? Take a few from daily life for a start:

Buying a business.
Building a shed.
Crossing a busy road.
Decorating a house.
Installing a heating system.

Too easy? What about that block of flats from Chapter 2? What sort of a building would emerge without knowing what should emerge? Now strangely enough most people will not argue about plans for a physical item. Most people agree that some sort of drawing or plan is necessary in order that a material object, whether simple or complex, can be manufactured. The interesting point is that very few people admit readily that management needs the same type of guidance in the form, not this time of a mechanical drawing, but of a definite plan. There is an increasing acceptance that good management is more a matter of science than ever it used to be and science in general builds upon a series of facts or accepted theories in order to advance.

Two of the prime requirements of good management are the ability and, sometimes more important, the will to plan. In dealing with the type of work which invariably demands a project management team with a Project Manager, it is absolutely essential to plan the work in the highest detail.

This plan must start with key technique 1, i.e. a proper identification of the task. The first job, therefore, of the Project Manager is to be sure that he knows what job he is to manage. This sounds common sense and of course it is; what perhaps distinguishes the first key technique from mere common sense is the depth of attack required.

The Objectives: Identification and Definition

There is, and always will be, a multitude of questions that cannot be answered precisely in the early stages of a project. This, however, will not prevent a knowledgeable and determined Project Manager from forcing to the surface the essential definition, so that the next steps in the project will be based upon the sound facts available at that time.

The rest of this chapter is based upon the project management of a highly successful southern England electronics company which, seriously considering the production of a new product, appointed a Project Manager to assist in evaluating it. If the company Board of Directors agree with the evaluation he is to carry out the full project management of the work.

In this case the first task was to put together the information from the Sales Manager and Research and Development Manager on which the idea of this particular project was based. The project management on this occasion was thus in the fullest business sense, and this is not always typical of project management in other companies. The function at this stage is often carried out by corporate planning organizations, especially in the larger companies. (In fact this particular company is now in the process of formalizing its corporate planning activities under a separate manager to coordinate the sales and other inputs into a corporate policy. The important step is that of formalizing—this is not to suggest there was no corporate policy before.)

The Project Manager's immediate action was to identify the type of system that was being proposed (key technique 1). He consulted with the functional managers and experts required, and from all the information gathered prepared a report.

Note that reports of this nature consist of a summary on which all the key information is in the form of a written report. It should conclude with a financial analysis in Discounted Cash Flow form (see Chapter 16). The report summary is then backed with further pages to give increasing detail.

Top management, as well as the Project Manager himself, must be able to refer virtually at a glance to the 'vital statistics' of the project. The whole aim is to *identify* the task in order that management may know clearly what risks they have to take and what reward can be expected for such risks. (See Project Choice, Chapter 18.) The whole report, and subsequent reports, should follow the principles of the project identification triangle, as displayed in Fig. 4.1.

The number of levels varies with the size and scope of the project and while four are shown, the number can obviously be more, but the levels must be sufficient to eventually get down to the smallest part of the whole project constitution. The project report must be built in the same way, with whatever detail can be obtained at the time. However, as is normal with any project, *full* details are never available until the project progresses.

The essence of all identification is the breakdown of work into dimensions; the time it takes, the resources needed, its place in the total work specification hierarchy. There is often quoted in books on work study and others the passage from Rudyard Kipling:

'I keep six honest serving men—They taught me all I know,
Their names are WHAT and WHY and WHEN and HOW and
WHERE and WHO'

It is very appropriate as well to project management!

Identify the WHO, WHAT, WHEN, HOW, WHERE, WHY of the project.

Before proceeding with an example of the report outline we should look at the top level key objectives.

The Top Level Key Objectives

In any project, while there is a multitude of activities comprising

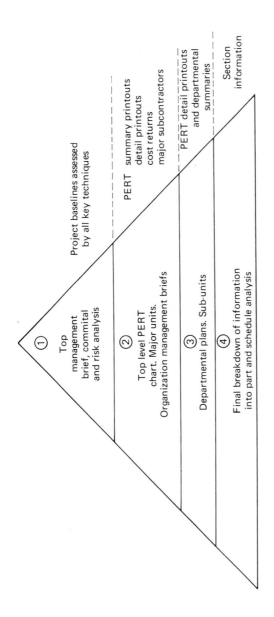

Fig. 4.1 The project identification triangle

① Top management brief, commital and risk analysis

Project baselines assessed by all key techniques

PERT summary printouts
detail printouts
cost returns
major subcontractors

② Top level PERT chart. Major units. Organization management briefs

③ Departmental plans. Sub-units

PERT detail printouts and departmental summaries

④ Final breakdown of information into part and schedule analysis

Section information

the total effort, there are in general only a few top level objectives which, when defined or specified correctly, set the scene of the project. Practically speaking, and going under different names in companies there are:

THE SYSTEMS CONCEPT STAGE—systems feasibility, concept feasibility, system aim, project aim, project formulation, etc.

THE PROJECT DEFINITION STAGE—system definition, project specification, job specification, etc.

DESIGN AND DEVELOPMENT STAGE—engineering, design and drawing, engineering development, etc.

MANUFACTURING STAGE—from pre-production to full production.

FIELD USAGE STAGE—Customer operational.

In each of these stages there has to be a fully defined and measurable specification. Without this, control is not possible; the project can easily slip to disaster, to a technical fiasco and financial loss. What this means in terms of preparation is that each key top level objective must have applied to it the key techniques.

In the first objective, i.e. the systems concept there must then be:

A full description of what we are trying to accomplish.
A full assessment of how we are going to achieve the task, the research, technical approach and technology required.
A full examination of the timescales and lower level key objectives as far as possible.
Complete cost estimates.
Definition of all resources and support in people and materials including the management of the project.

In the other objectives a similar series of statements must be made. Items particular to each stage (without repeating common issue areas) are:

PROJECT DEFINITION A full specification of the product including separate specifications for major units, especially bought out items. Specification includes drawings, sketches and pictures to help fully specify the product.

DESIGN AND DEVELOPMENT STAGE Building of prototypes; proving of prototypes to the full specification now evolved, i.e. a design review; feasibility of manufacturing the product; design changes if necessary.

MANUFACTURING Proving of production engineering; proving the product cost; design and process changes if necessary.

FIELD USAGE Field reports on breakdowns; statistical work by quality assurance and design changes if necessary.

What we have, therefore, as a common pattern applicable to all projects is a three dimensional picture of project drive to fruition. One dimension is the project thrust through the key baselines or objectives; a second dimension is the application throughout of all key objectives; the third dimension is the line function skills applicable all through and measured by the key techniques.

While the evaluation report over the next few pages is an example of a manufactured product designed to be product line, the principles hold good for other types of work where a central technical and managerial interface must be created. (The DCF report is not included as the subject is covered in Chapter 16.)

Evaluation Report

In this section is set out a fairly typical evaluation report.

EVALUATION REPORT NO. 23 MAGNETIC TAPE TRANSPORT CA314

1.0 SYSTEMS CONCEPT

General Description

A new version of the highly successful self-contained transport CA300 is envisaged. The new features are:

16 tracks instead of 10.

200 inches second speed instead of 120 inches second

new method of recording (our project RR34)

new servo system

crystal power supplies

electronic circuitry to new company range of

20 strata crystalsor circuits.

The unit will be capable of receiving, storing and transmitting data over high speed lines.

The risks of the project are principally in the servo system, based upon the plastic drag clutch being developed by Premier Plastic Products Ltd. Any degradation of this item will seriously affect the speed capability.

Marketing

The market research shows a clear market for this device in the bureau interchange field. Estimated sales are 2500 over 5 years starting in 1973. The market research has covered all of Europe over the last 10 months. The sales price should be set at about £50K.

Development and Manufacture

The systems concept seen so far envisages the development timescale as:

TO Specification baseline .. .. 4 months from start
TO Development
    proving of prototype .. .. 12 months
    manufacturing model .. .. 14 months
    release of drawings .. .. 16 months

TO Manufacture
    first batch of 20 machines   ..   21 months
    second batch of 50 machines
    proving all drawings, processes
    and costs ..   ..   23 months
TO First customer ..   ..   ..   25 months
(Note: Reports on all new developments and state of research are attached as further appendices together with evidence of progress.)

2.0 RESOURCES (KEY TECHNIQUE 2)

Finance

A Discounted Cash Flow statement at the end of this report summary, together with risk analysis summaries, shows the effects of late start, higher costs and lack of progress on all the costs listed in this report. On the assumptions made, the project will show a minimum 17 per cent DCF rate of return.

Human Effort

As will be shown in detail in the appendices, projects P39 and P53 are now nearly completed. Professional design effort for the specification stage is thus available.

The Quality Control Organization will require 12 extra testers in about 12 months.

Special consideration must be given to Customer Engineering Organization personnel training in the crystalsor circuits and the plastic drag clutch operation. It is not yet known how many of the present staff are capable of this work training, but it is thought there will be sufficient.

In manufacturing, there will be a need for 10 men in the printed circuit manufacturing plant, plus 20 women.

Materials and Equipment

While it is reflected in the DCF summaries, there will be prototype units for the transport to order now from the specialist subcontractors. This will involve an immediate commitment of £30K.

Additional plant is required for the electronic circuit production. This is required in 14 months' time, to be ordered in 5 months and will cost £25K.

E

Special test equipment for Quality Control and Quality Assurance will amount to £50K. £7K will need to be committed in 2 months, the balance of £43K in 5 months.

Services
There are additional printed circuit facilities which will require extensions of the present effluent tanks and water supply in factory No. 2A.

3.0 TIMESCALES (KEY TECHNIQUE 3)
Apart from the system concept level of dates shown in (1.0) above, some breakdowns occur in the appendices for each of the line function organizations.

4.0 QUALITY AND RELIABILITY
Many of these units will be on 24 hour usage and the reliability must be very high—aiming point to be a mean time between failure of 20,000 hours. Maintenance will be carried out on a standby device basis.

We have no doubts about the crystalsor circuits, the crystal power supplies or the method of recording, but the prototype servo system mechanics will at the moment only achieve 5000 hours m.t.b.f. In those cases with redundant standby device conditions we are satisfied since the repair time can be very rapid and less than the minimum changeover time of devices. This servo reliability will be attacked as a major item, but the risk exists on about 30 per cent of all the predicted sales.

5.0 PRODUCT COST
The first estimates, including production engineering and special development amortized over the sales figures, set a works cost of about £20K per unit.

Appendix 1 to Evaluation Report No. 23   **Sheet 1/1**

SALES REPORT ON NEW TAPE TRANSPORT CA 314

Sales report detailing marketing aspects as briefly stated on front sheet

Sales by area, district and type of customer—tables by years' anticipated sales

Quantity and percentage of total market

Explanation of pricing structure

Competition effects and effects upon competition.

Effect on present range of products

Fit of new product in present range

Advertising—samples—seminars—
customer courses—requirements.

Finance

Changes to budgets—new budget preparation.

Effects on other budgets.

Any capital expenditure.

Human Effort

Changes in sales force by type or number.

Management and supervision—total effort.

Organization changes.

Training.

Materials and Equipment

Training aids—packing and transportation.

Space

Sales offices—sufficient facilities or not?

Services

Are existing services sufficient?

Timescales

For training—advertising programme.

Sales and placing of first production models.

51

Appendix 2 to Evaluation Report No. 23　　　　　　**Sheet 2/1**

ENGINEERING REPORT ON NEW TAPE TRANSPORT CA314

Finance

Changes to budgets—New budget preparation.

Effects on other products.

Special sums for materials or equipment, bought out, made in, home or overseas.

Special mention of worst risks in research, new techniques and extension of present techniques.

Any output in prototypes or early models.

Capital expenditure requirements.

Human Effort

Research requirements.

New techniques.

Extension of existing techniques.

Existing techniques.

Changes or additions of types and numbers of staff-management and supervision—Total effort.

Effects on other products.

In terms of major units.

Product after sales support.

Any training effects.

Specification of project baselines.

Materials and Equipment

Special materials, major bought out units from home and overseas for development and research.

Test equipment for laboratory and research work.

Space

Are existing laboratory facilities sufficient?

Is building, test and 'think' room large enough?

Does this mean rearrangements, extra buildings?

Services

Are existing services sufficient?

Timescales

Key plan showing all major events and baselines.

Appendix 3 to Evaluation Report No. 23

PRODUCT SPECIFICATION

In this section of the original report there was a detailed specification of the tape transport. This is specific to one industry and so we will not repeat it but we will set down more general guidelines which can apply to a number of industries. It would be impossible to promise that all items are included, but you should be able to develop further ideas from the following list.

What does a product specification have to do? We will set down a series of questions; the answers will comprise the skeleton of a specification; more words, details, pictures and diagrams are needed to fully produce the specification.

What is it?
    A road?
    A block of flats?
    A bridge?
    An electronic device?

What does it do?
    Carry people—traffic—goods?
    House families—bachelors—nurses?
    Measure voltage—frequency—light?
    Read marks—print letters?

What does it look like?
    Shape—round—square—boxlike—squat—tall?
    Size—width—length—height?
    Colour?
    Style—ornate—simple?
    Weight—heavy—light?
    All to be described qualitatively and quantitatively.

What is it made of?
    Steel—aluminium—wood—concrete?
    Girders—sheet steel—bar—tube?

Is it one piece or several major units?
    One very large—two small?
    What do *they* look like?
    Are there pictures, illustrations, diagrams, sketches, plans?

How does it do what it does?
Then follows the intimate detail appropriate to the device, object, etc. A definition of the technical terms likely to be found is usually essential in this section or at the beginning of the specification.

Does it need services to function?
Electricity—gas—oil?
Telephone—telegraph—private wire?
Water—drainage—air?

What is the specification for these services?
Single phase—three phase?
Volts amps—voltage—frequency?
Hard—soft—pressure?
Surges—low—high?
Effects of interruptions.

Does the product produce anything?
Electrical interference—signals—pictures?
Readings, audio sounds, heat, cold?
Water, effluent.
Paper, print, liquid.
Specify these.

Are there limiting factors to the function?
Environment—heat—cold—wetness—dryness?
Air cleanliness?
Vibration—weight—electrical interference.
Variations of services (electricity—gas, etc.)
Surges?
Fine limits of manufacture? Adjustments in use?
Special selection of parts?
Special specifications for consumable items?

What maintenance must be provided?
Hours per day, week, month, period?
Adjustments, per time period?
Special settings?

Replacements of parts, minor or major units?
Costs? Total over (n) years.
Accessibility?

Does the product require consumable items?
Water—oil—paper—card—copy ribbon?
Costs per period or operation?

What is the likely production cost with what quantities?
What packing and transit instructions are there?
Are there special environmental conditions for transit or
storage? Heat—cold—wet—dry?
One way up?
Vibration—shock?
Air—ship—rail—road.

Does the product have any relationship to other products in the
company range of competition?
Is there any standard interface to other products?
Plugs, sockets, exits, entrances, signs?
Are there country, European, world standards applicable?

Are there accessories necessary or supplied?
Is there special test equipment required?
For all of it? Part of it?

Can the product be enhanced?
Bigger—better—more powerful?
Longer—more reliable—better value?

What is the reliability?
Mean time between breakdowns?
Maintenance intervals.

What failures are likely?
Can they be detected?
Do they merely reduce productivity?
Can they be put right without interruption?
What interruption times are envisaged?

Will any overseas items be required or major subcontract units?
They will need to be specified fully!
Is any licensing required?

Does the product need drivers, minders or operators?
Is their task specified?

Have safety precautions been specified?
Is the necessary safety design included?
The specification must have a change notice sheet in the front to record the changes, when, what, by whom, approved by whom and on each sheet must be an issue number of the specification.

Appendix 4 to Evaluation Report No. 23

MANUFACTURING AND OTHER REPORTS ON NEW TAPE TRANSPORT
CA314
This appendix and others followed the pattern of appendix 1 and 2
and there would be much duplication to repeat it. The main concern
was to express in resources and timescales the effects of introducing
the new product. Some items peculiar to manufacturing and other
organizations concerned are:

Manufacturing
Development costs (preproduction models and production
engineering)
Introduction costs (learning curves)
Capital costs—(plant—tools—jigs—equipment).

Quality Assurance
Prototypes for QA tests.

Quality Control
Preproduction units for training.
Factory test gear development.

Customer Engineering
Special test equipment development for field servicing.

part two The Essential Steps

five Getting down to Business

THE REPORT SHAPE IN Chapter 4 included the major headings of a business plan as well as a detailed definition of the new product. Business planning is not the prime subject of this volume and the company in question did decide to proceed. The Project Manager was authorized to get the task started in a proper manner. He had in this project the great advantage of being in at the beginning—so often the Project Manager is brought in too late after many decisions have already been taken; he then may have a millstone round his neck. It is fair to say, however, that in those enlightened companies who use project management properly this does not happen. The Project Manager is either brought in to do the job we are describing, at the beginning, or he is brought in to work with the company corporate product planners.

Initial Organization

An organization must now be set up appropriate to the size of the project; many projects will involve perhaps only the Project Manager and a secretary as 'the project management'. Others will involve a project management team, the Project Manager, secretary and key assistant managers. It is not possible to give rules because there are none; it very much depends upon the interpretation of the picture presented to top management by the facts as known (Fig. 5.1).

Fig. 5.1 Determination of project organization

In this case a Project Manager and secretary approach was sufficient and will adequately illustrate the techniques we must use. A larger team deals with more of the same techniques and the Project Manager is likely to be biased more towards the business side of project management as distinct from the technical (see Chapter 3).

The Essential Steps

Key technique 1. Define the Task

But we have defined it you may argue, we have written a detailed report (Chapter 4).

But to whom? A rather select few so far. We said in Chapter 3:

'One of the most important responsibilities, however, of a Project Manager is to ensure that all parties, from their respective functional operations or subcontract basis, have a clear, unambiguous and common understanding of the project, its aims and complete purpose. This aspect,

61

apart from any other, is always instrumental in ensuring the highest chance of a successful project for the company.'

The first task then for the Project Manager was to talk with the managers and appropriate staff in order to discuss thoroughly the project definition and make the job clear to all. In these discussions, the next key techniques were brought to bear.

Key Technique 2. Resources

This breaks down into five areas:

FINANCE

Notwithstanding the business plan report, budgets must be now assessed in the light of the most up to date information and modified to include the new product, and it is very important that these budgets are prepared as accurately as possible. The Project Manager must ensure they are based upon correct information about the project, including an assumed feasible timescale.

As soon as possible, through the proper management chain, the comprehensive budget will appear. This must be approved by the Managing Director and the project is then 'legal!'.

Note that the budgets are modified: there must always be in existence a long term budget, say 3 to 4 years, and a short term budget, usually 12 months. Finance under such a system when coupled with measurements of actual performance is under control.

Some examples of budgeting procedures taken from the case study in Chapter 4 are shown in Figs. 5.2 and 5.3.

The Project Manager should then see that the company Accounting Department prepares an overall project budget and expenditure summary as a control account. Figure 5.4 shows an example which should be able to be produced by mechanization of one kind or another every month. It shows the variances against period budget and expenditure. In most companies the accounts will be on a line function basis with variances per functional organization brought to light each period or month. What may not be revealed in a multi-project organization is the contribution each project makes to the total.

There is of course difficulty in this in that projects may share the advantage of new or existing machinery in a given cost centre. Companies will solve this sort of problem in their own way, but there can be no excuse, even in severe function line accounting, for the Project Manager not attempting to cost and monitor the project costs.

In the budgeting will be included the results of examining the other facets of key technique 2, i.e. manpower, materials, equipment, space and services. There will be, subsidiary to the main cash flow of the project as a whole, sub-cash flows to justify, say, this or that type of equipment. Like all project processes the concept of the equipment comes first, with costs as revealed in the concept stage. As the project passes to the specification stage, and beyond, so a closer look can be taken at all costs. Budgeting and cost justifications must be a continuous process to optimize the value of the project.

Example of engineering budget application for whole or part of the project

Short title of work					Indicate project type
Labour and overheads	Year			Total	
	1	2	3		
Workshops					Project development ☐
Sheet metal					
Equipment design					Product improvement ☐
Electro-mechanics					
Technical services					Research and techniques ☐
Design drawing					
Tactical					Other* ☐
Electronics					
Research					Project number
Total labour (A)					
Materials	╱	╱	╱		Customer
Purchases					
Subcontracts					*Describe
Other engineering divisions					
Other company divisions					
Product line items					
Total materials (B)					
Total estimate (A) + (B)					
Work in progress					
Output					

Description of work

Budget application prepared by: Approvals

. . . .

Line Manager . . . .   General

Project Manager . . . .   Manager . . . .

Fig. 5.2 Example of budget application

Period cost statement

Short title of work   Project number   Period number   Engineer   Ended / /

	Branch	Current period	Previous periods	Total
Labour and overheads	Workshops			
	Sheet metal			
	Equipment design			
	Electromechanics			
	Technical services			
	Design drawing			
	Tactical			
	Electronics			
	Research			
	Total labour			
Materials	Purchases			
	Subcontracts			
	Other engineering divisions			
	Other company divisions			
	Product line items			
	Total materials			
	Total expenditure			

History of expenditure

	Totals
Year	
Estimate	
Actual	
% actual/estimate	
Estimate output	
Actual output	
Brief comments	
Signature	

Fig. 5.3 Example of period cost statement

F

Project budget and expenditure summary (revenue)				
Division or organization	Type of expenditure	Budget year/month/ period	Expenditure year/month/ period	Variance year/month/ period
Research	Manpower Materials TOTAL			
Engineering	Development Prototype build TOTAL			
Quality assurance	Planning Product approval Tests TOTAL			

Manufacturing	Development
	Planning
	Introduction costs
	          Product
	          Services
	                TOTAL			

Quality control	Test and inspection Procedures Excess test costs TOTAL			
Project management	Manpower Other costs TOTAL			
Other areas	 TOTAL			
	GRAND TOTALS			

Capital requirements
    Research
    Engineering
    Quality assurance
    Manufacturing
    Quality control
    Project management
    Other areas
                TOTALS				

Fig. 5.4 Example of summary budget and expenditure sheet

While Figs 5.2 and 5.3 are for engineering budgets, similar budgets are prepared for all other line functions. In common with all project management technique procedures, the budgets should be prepared on a specification 'tree' basis, i.e. not only

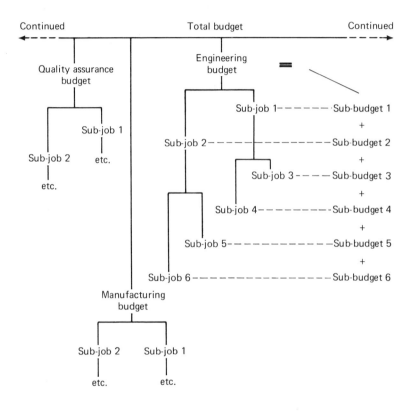

Fig. 5.5 Budget breakdown principle

the financial budgets, but all the remaining items in key technique 2 are treated in the 'breakdown tree' manner. The breakdown of each sub-job has its own key technique 2 items, i.e. manpower, materials, equipment, etc. in each smallest sub-job.

MANPOWER

In carrying out the budget preparation, a manpower budget will also have to be completed. The finance budget may well allow an amount per man based upon averages adjusted from time to time. The manpower budget applies itself to types of people who must be involved, e.g. specialists in any area, supervisors or managers. It should also show clearly the build up of staff on this project and effects on other projects in the assumed timescale.

While lists and quantities of people are adequate (Fig. 5.6) a manpower build up chart is often useful (Fig. 5.7).

Type		\multicolumn{15}{c	}{Months or chosen periods}
		1	2	3	4	5	6	7	8	9	10	11	12	13	14	15
6	Prototype wiremen	−	−	−	1	1	2	2	3	3	3	3	3	3	3	3
5	Production engineers	1	1	1	1	1	1	2	2	2	2	3	3	3	3	3
4	Circuit engineers	1	1	1	2	2	2	2	2	1	1	1	1	1	1	1
3	Logic designers	1	1	2	2	2	3	3	3	3	2	2	1	1	1	1
2	System designers	3	3	3	3	2	2	1	1	−	−	−	−	−	−	−
1	Project management	2	2	2	2	2	2	2	2	2	2	2	2	2	2	2
	TOTAL	8	8	9	11	10	12	12	13	11	10	11	10	10	10	10

Fig. 5.6 Manpower list

Effects on other projects can be noted in a similar manner to Fig. 5.8, i.e. reprepare their manpower requirements. This may also cause effects in timescales and costs. General management will seek out from the project managers these effects and balance the project priorities accordingly. It is a fact that with several projects on the move the manpower is the item usually most difficult to manoeuvre. It is, apart from 'bulk buying' during takeovers, a much more fixed resource when talking of professional and technical staff, than even money. While overtrading, with its sometimes calamitous financial effects, is well

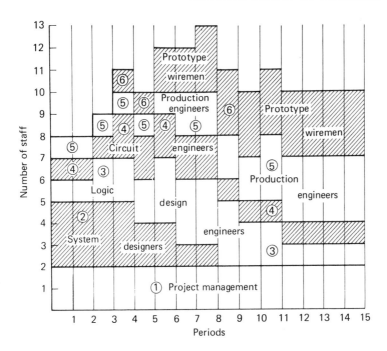

Fig. 5.7 Manpower chart

understood, manpower over- and undertrading seems not so well understood. To recruit a man is fairly easy, to ensure he is the right man is difficult, to train him in a short time is even more difficult. Even with skilled and experienced personnel it may be several months before they are really at top efficiency and getting the most out of any staff they have.

A simple staff/project card system could be as Fig. 5.8, enabling a ready check on project staffing.

MATERIALS AND EQUIPMENT
In the preparation of the budget, with knowledge of the time-scale and manpower requirements we shall also need to define the material and equipment types, costs and arrival times.

In terms of materials the first risks may now have to be assumed. Up to now, no actual cash has been spent, except on

69

the feasibility report and budget preparations. To a large extent these are 'overhead items' and will occur inside the company again. Now, however, the Project Manager must, after careful

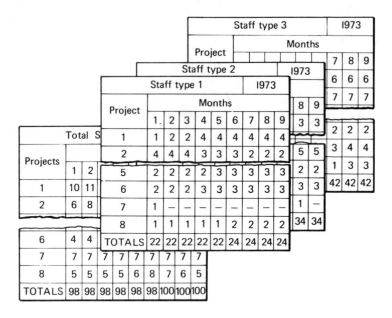

Fig. 5.8 Manpower overall staffing picture

examination of the detailed plans prepared, sanction the ordering of any long delivery items. The risk is twofold, financial in the sense that the wrong materials may prove to have been ordered in the light of subsequent experience and secondly that time may be wasted in obtaining the correct materials if a mistake has been made. Materials will include both raw materials and partly finished or fully finished items. Ordering is dictated by the timescale, the money involved and the possible risks.

In terms of equipment this will cover the same sort of risks as for materials. The timescale together with the risks involved will dictate the ordering times. Equipment will cover special equipment for early engineering development, manufacturing process development or test equipment development.

In examining the necessity for such orders it is essential to have had the timescale and logic of the plan thoroughly vetted as there is no point in buying materials and equipment before it is absolutely necessary. The effects of not ordering must be well known—there may be a way round the problem until the Project Manager is more certain of the items he requires. The cost of waste on the other hand may be less than the cost of delays.

A careful record must be kept of material expenditure and a simple budget and expenditure chart like Fig. 5.9 will suffice; better still, the information will be provided from the accounting system or data bank set up for the project.

Project :	Project number		
Budget £	Class of materials		
Date	Item bought	Amount	Balance

Fig. 5.9 Material control form

Graphical information can be provided similar to capital budget records for equipment (see below).

CAPITAL BUDGETS

Since capital is treated very differently to revenue in the company accounts it is necessary to log it separately. Apart from capital expenditure approvals and records, it is useful to have a capital budget and expenditure graph. On this graph can also be put committed figures because often an order for capital equipment is placed many months ahead. If a project has to be closed down it is essential to know what is committed as well as actually paid for. Even if the plant or other capital goods can be cancelled there are likely to be cancellation charges. A budget control graph example is drawn in Fig. 5.10.

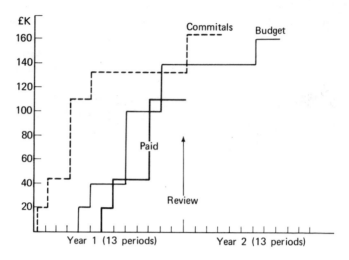

Fig. 5.10 Capital control graph

SPACE

The effects of the project may mean no changes in the provision of overall space, or it may mean new laboratories, new works, test areas or extensions to existing facilities. Space requirement is a function of added plant and equipment, manufacturing lines, test space, manpower facilities and the like. This means that adequate knowledge of these items must be available before space requirements can be properly calculated. The main function of the Project Manager is again to see that the line managers are well aware of all the project's likely demand, as inadequate space will lead to inefficiency if not an impossible situation.

The type of space which may not have been anticipated is somewhere to bring together a large complex system or proto-type prior to shipping or for test purposes. The latter may be particularly applicable if a large system has to be tested prior to despatch for customer approval tests and demonstrations. This may be unusual for the company and it could easily get left too late for comfort! Space could also be necessary in the form of temporary building to house large units on site prior to final siting.

SERVICES AND FACILITIES

The normal facilities of electricity, gas and water are fairly straightforward, at least in terms of factories, laboratories and the like; the complications set in when one considers a chemical factory or metal processing plant. In such cases one might need new roads, even a new electricity generating station and perhaps port facilities. Notwithstanding the increased size and scope of the task the key techniques cover all instances.

Key Technique 3. Timescale

Some Project Managers prefer to follow key technique 1 by 3 instead of 2 as we have done. In fact 2 and 3 are so interdependent that while we describe them separately it is certain that much interplay will take place.

Using PERT methods about which we comment in Chapter 11 a time plan of work must be drawn up.

Circulate to the line managers what appears now to be the key event date requirements to enable the project to be completed. Completion is either agreed by top management to be a customer stated date, in which case we must say so, or the end date is what we believe will be both politically acceptable and feasible.

Request the line managers to have prepared their detailed plans of their activities together with reasons for any divergence from the key plan. The key plan can be simply a list of dates as Fig. 5.11 or a line plan Fig. 5.12. There is little to choose and perhaps the simple list is more readily adjustable.

During this process the Project Manager will be spending much time with the appropriate staff who are drawing up the plans, not to influence their decisions at this stage but to make sure there is no doubt in any mind as to what the project task really is.

In time for revisions and approval by the Project Manager and

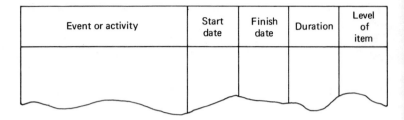

Event or activity	Start date	Finish date	Duration	Level of item

Fig. 5.11 List of key events

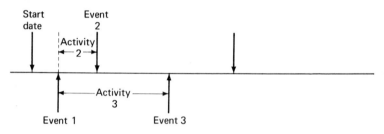

Fig. 5.12 Line of key events

top management, the plans of all organizations and departments come together. The plans can be integrated, i.e. no separation of functional organization, Fig. 5.13 or the functional responsibilities can be clarified, Fig. 5.14.

The latter method is not very convenient and becomes confusing for even a few activities unless much time is spent on rearrangements. It is certainly possible to avoid the 'dummy' zero time activities we have used to join up the departmental activities. If PERT is used in conjunction with a computer all the departmental groups of activities are obtainable quite simply as printouts.

As soon as possible, the complete logic of the plan must be checked and agreed with all responsible managers, and as a matter of urgency after that the complete plan must either be computer run or hand calculated to give all dates in a tabulated form; key dates must be separately extracted and bar charts can also be usefully extracted from the PERT process.

At this stage of the project, speed is essential in feeding back the appropriate information to organization and departmental managers, because it is certain the timescales and resources will not be in harmony. This 'round the course' action may have to be carried out two or three times until all line management, top management and project management are in unison and are convinced that they have a feasible minimum risk plan, within the budgets laid down.

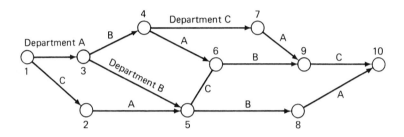

Fig. 5.13 Simple PERT chart

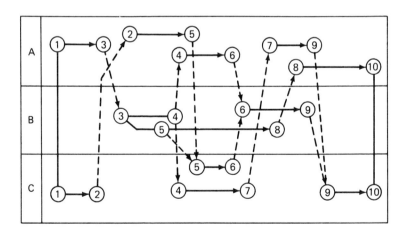

Fig. 5.14 PERT chart, by departments

75

The Interplay between Timescales and Resources

Figure 5.15 shows a simplified network for the installation of a heating system. Figures in brackets after the number of weeks in the activity are the number of hot water fitters required. Figure 5.16 after the PERT chart gives the normal PERT information; the thick line on the diagram is the critical path and against each event is written the earliest (E) and latest (L) event times.

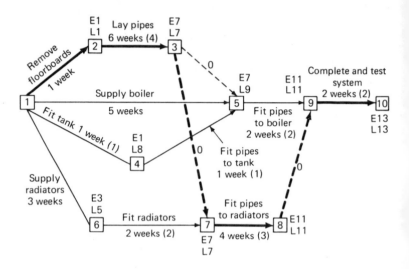

Fig. 5.15 PERT chart, for resource calculations

If any reader is not familiar with PERT there are a few comments about Figs. 5.15 and 5.16 that will be helpful. The earliest times E, E7, etc. on the chart are calculated by adding up the activity weeks from the start, down each path. When two or more activities arrive at an event, e.g. event 5 in Fig. 5.15 the highest total of weeks is carried forward to calculate the next earliest times, i.e. at event 5 the input path totals are, from event 3, —7 weeks, from event 1, —5 weeks, and from event 4, —2 weeks, hence 7 weeks is carried forward. From event 5 to event 9 is 2 weeks, but the earliest time at event 9 is not $7+2 = 9$ but 11. This is because activity 8 to 9 is also an input and is carrying forward an earliest time of 11.

Activity	Duration weeks	Start time		Finish time		Float			Number of fitters per week	Note
		Early	Late	Early	Late	Total	Free	Ind.		
1 to 2	1	0	0	1	1	0	0	0	—	Critical path item
1 to 4	1	0	0	1	8	7	0	0	1	
1 to 5	5	0	0	7	9	4	2	2	—	
1 to 6	3	0	0	3	5	2	0	0	—	
2 to 3	6	1	1	7	7	0	0	0	4	Critical path item
3 to 5	0	7	7	7	9	2	0	0	—	Dummy: restraint
3 to 7	0	7	7	7	7	0	0	0	—	Critical path: restraint
4 to 5	1	1	8	7	9	7	5	−2	1	
5 to 9	2	7	9	11	11	2	2	0	2	
6 to 7	2	3	5	7	7	2	2	0	2	
7 to 8	4	7	7	11	11	0	0	0	3	Critical path item
8 to 9	0	11	11	11	11	0	0	0	—	Critical path: restraint
9 to 10	2	11	11	13	13	0	0	0	2	Critical path item
Col. 1	Col. 2	Col. 3	Col. 4	Col. 5	Col. 6	Col. 7 = Col. 6 − Col. 3 − Col. 2	Col. 8 = Col. 5 − Col. 3 − Col. 2	Col. 9 = Col. 5 − Col. 4 − Col. 2		

Fig. 5.16 Table of information from Fig. 5.15

The critical path is that path with the highest totals of earliest times carried forward. This should be evident from Fig. 5.15.

To calculate the latest times we start at the end of the task, i.e. event 10 in this instance, and work backwards subtracting the activity times. The difficulty, if any, in this occurs at events not on the critical path. The critical path events will show the same latest and earliest times. In our example, an apparent difficulty might be at event 5 to event 3 where the late time at event 5 is 9 weeks, the activity from 5 to 3 is zero but the latest time at event 3 is 7 weeks. The reason for this is that in the same way as we took the higher figures going forward, so we take the lower figures going backwards where two or more activities occur at the same event.

77

Having obtained the earliest and latest times it is then fairly simple to fill in the table in Fig. 5.16. The earliest start is simply the E time at the start of the activity. The earliest finish is the E time at the end of the activity. The latest start and finish is the L time.

The float times are those number of weeks that an activity can 'float' between an early start and a late finish, without affecting the total time of the project; this is set by the critical path where no float exists.

The total float is calculated by subtracting the activity time from the difference between the earliest start and latest finish of the activity.

The free float is calculated by subtracting the difference between the earliest and latest finish times from the total float.

The independent float is calculated by subtracting the difference between the earliest and latest start from the free float.

The significance of these various calculations is twofold. From a

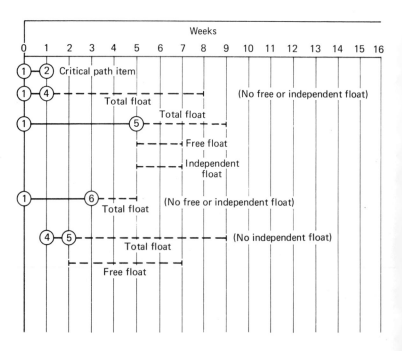

Fig. 5.17 Activity floats

time point of view it is vital to know which tasks are critical and must not be late, as opposed to those activities where it is possible to adjust their time length or position in time without affecting the overall project time. To provide further clarity Fig. 5.17 shows some of the activities from Fig. 5.15, their place in time and their various floats.

The other need for the float calculations is to be able to plan the resources correctly. If we now draw a bar chart of the activities and men employed, we can sum the weekly demands and also draw a histogram of the fitters required (Fig. 5.18).

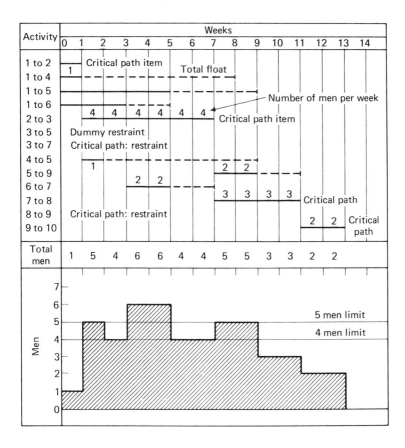

Fig. 5.18 Bar chart and manpower histogram

If, however, the number of fitters is limited to 5 in total, how does this affect the timescale of the whole job? First draw a line across at the 5 men level. The overload is in weeks 4 and 5 of one fitter each week. What can we do? There is more than one solution but the first job is to try and remove non-critical path effort to reduce the overload. Unfortunately, activity 6 to 7 has only 2 weeks' free float and if we started it 2 weeks late to take up the float it merely transfers the overload to weeks 5 and 6. However, if one man could work on his own each week, instead of 2 men in weeks 3 and 4, we could put 1 man in each of the weeks 3, 4, 5 and 6. If this is not acceptable then activity 2 to 3 would have to suffer, e.g. 1 man removed from weeks 3 to 4 causing an extension to the whole project by 2 man weeks. (If 4 men were used $-\frac{1}{2}$ week in total time.)

What now if 4 men is the limit? There are overloads in weeks 2, 4, 5, 8 and 9, so a rescheduling operation has to be carried out. It is clear from the previous 5 men limit that the overall project time is going to be exceeded if the estimates per week are accurate. Again, it appears that activity 2 to 3 is the only one likely to yield an improvement by lowering the men per week. There are likely to be several solutions and the usual procedure is to try what appears to be possible, draw the histogram and then see if a better solution can be seen. However, once the timetable is altered then all or any of the floats can change giving yet other solutions. By a series of 'best' efforts, a solution can be found which appears to be optimum. It may not actually be the optimum but the laws of diminishing returns will soon apply, coupled with the fact that all the estimates are bound to have some tolerance in them. For example, if we construct a new table with less effort per week in activity 2 to 3 it could be as Fig. 5.19. This shows several alterations to other activities and a project overrun of $1\frac{2}{3}$ weeks.

The resources problem for one project can be taken further when several projects are competing for the same type of staff. In all the work involved with manpower resources the aim is to minimize delay, minimize costs and lower the staff requirements.

Another kind of optimization is a simple smoothing of requirements. Notwithstanding the timescales and numbers of staff, it is not reasonable, let alone possible, to have large fluctuations of staff from week to week, e.g. Fig. 5.20, shaded plus white.

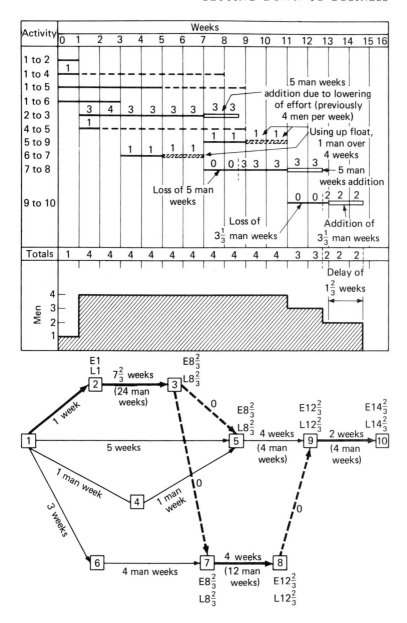

Fig. 5.19 Revised Fig. 5.18 and corresponding PERT chart

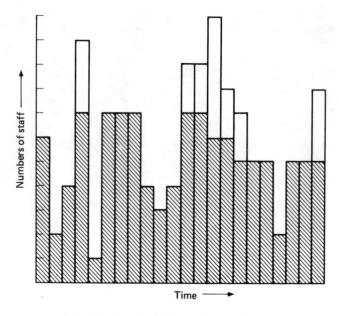

Fig. 5.20 Manpower demand smoothing

Such a picture requires smoothing to an acceptable level—the shaded level only, say,—plus filling the remaining 'holes' as well as can be achieved. This is but an example and there will be many solutions.

six Quality and Reliability

KEY TECHNIQUE 4 ASKS THE QUESTION 'What quality and reliability have to be achieved?' The knowledge of whether we have performed a task to the standards we or other bodies may have set down only comes after a long period of use in the actual environment of the project or product use. However, to give the maximum chance of achieving these laid down standards certain defined steps have to be taken in a company to ensure success. Quality tests may be the last visible checks that the company can take to check the work quality, but long before this time arrives much foundation work must be done.

Quality Assurance

The first step on the road to whatever quality and reliability we have decided is to set down detailed specifications in order that all people engaged in the project shall know to what standards of quality we have decided to work. For example, we might argue that if we used, say, stainless steel or copper to make a component box inside an electronic unit the quality is better than sheet mild steel which might have done the job. However, the cost to the company would be totally unnecessary as it would not improve the functional operation of the equipment, would probably not be seen and, therefore, could not be claimed as a selling point and was a complete waste of money. On the other hand, if the various parts of the equipment were held together with pieces of rough string, we would all agree that this was carrying economy too far and that we would not be likely to sell many, if any, of such units. The quality would be too low. If one now considers all the many, many items comprising any piece of equipment, there is obviously a path to be chosen all through the equipment with unnecessarily high quality on the one hand, and too poor a quality on the other. Standards have had to be laid down at all stages. This is the job of Quality Assurance. Bound up with quality is reliability. It does not always follow that high quality implies effective reliability, but it now depends on what we mean. For example, if an electronic component is supposed to withstand a continual stated voltage across it, then it is fairly certain that a component chosen to withstand, say, 20 per cent more than the applied voltage will last longer. On the other hand a higher quality

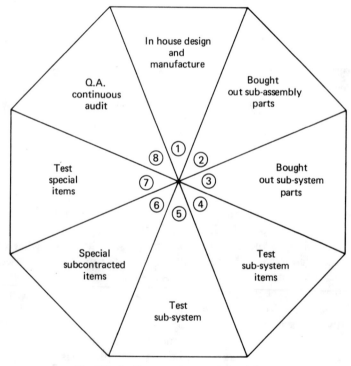

Fig. 6.1 Quality assurance work breakdown

product in terms of materials may fail if it is only just capable of doing the job required of it. Again, therefore, the 'quality' of all parts has to be assessed in these terms; how long will the part last before replacement. Too high a reliability costs money in the first instance and loses customers because of the initial price. Too low a reliability loses customers for the future after they have tried you once! Maintenance costs rise and usefulness decreases. As well as the choice of the quality and reliability of every component in the system, which will determine in the end the price, the life and the selling appeal of the equipment, the Quality Assurance Department must prepare a series of tests which will do two things. The first is to operate the equipment, whatever it may be, in conditions which are equal to, or greater than, the worst conditions the equipment is specified for, over a period of time which will enable the reliability figures to be ascertained to a high degree of confidence. The second series of tests must be those which can be carried out under factory conditions, rather than the worst conditions, and from which quality control figures can be obtained for product output.

Where does Quality Assurance fit in to the project management picture? Most projects comprise a mixture of skills and apart from the proportions of each, Fig. 6.1 illustrates a typical breakdown of project main areas.

IN HOUSE ITEMS

This can mean either standard product line items that the company manufactures or it can mean a special item for this particular project. It is exceedingly likely that the Quality Assurance group will require no prodding to make sure that the item is 'quality assured'. However, the Project Manager, particularly with the specially manufactured item, must make quite sure that Quality Assurance are carrying out all the normal functions they carry out with the product line items. Indeed, there may be information that the Project Manager can supply to them in terms of the function and working environment of the equipment.

BOUGHT OUT SUB-ASSEMBLY PARTS

These can cover a very wide range from single, simple components to fairly complex sub-assemblies. With regard to the ordinary components, the company which is of longish standing in the field will probably already possess standard quality assurance procedures which can be applied or extrapolated to include any new parts. In the case of the more complex part, it may well be that Quality Assurance have to investigate more thoroughly and plan inspection and test procedures for these parts, in order that the standards of quality and reliability of the company are met in the part under consideration.

BOUGHT OUT SUB-SYSTEM ITEMS

In some respects these are the more complete 'top end' items of the previous section, and in the electronic field one could compare, for example, in item 2 a multiple capacitor block, which is somewhat beyond the single simple component, with a complete power supply in the item 3 and 4 section. In this latter case, the Quality Assurance group have certainly to investigate, especially if large quantities are involved, the standing of the manufacturer who is to supply the completed item, his ability to supply the quantities from a manufacturer who is to supply the completed item, his ability to supply the quantities from a manufacturing capacity and financial resource point of view. These are somewhat delicate matters and require people in Quality Assurance who can talk to manufacturers and obtain the information in an open manner, and without giving any offence. It is unfortunate that many subcontractors do not feel that these enquiries are any business of the main contractor, whereas, in fact, they are exceedingly important to both parties. The multiple stores certainly look carefully into quality, standing and ability to supply of their suppliers and the better multiples help their suppliers in many ways. Having satisfied themselves that the supplier is able to supply in the fullest sense, then Quality Assurance must also look carefully at the specification of the sub-system item, evolve suitable environmental tests and completely assure themselves and the project that the sub-system item is indeed capable of operating to the specification, both in terms of function and in terms of reliability over the necessary time periods. Bound up inextricably with this process is their constant regard for the general quality of the product.

Once these procedures have been derived, then tests on representative samples can be made, and only when these have been satisfactorily concluded can the Project Manager really believe that he has a sub-system item which will be suitable for the project.

SPECIAL SUBCONTRACTED ITEMS

These items are, in many ways, much worse than the previous items we have just talked about, as the specification for such an item is often of a development nature, whereas the example given above, e.g. a power supply, may well be based upon very sound and usual design principles. In the case of these special subcontracted items, the Project Manager has a very great degree of responsibility to see that key technique 1 is fully adhered to, i.e. define the task thoroughly. Unless this is done there will be a grave likelihood of either not receiving what the project really requires, and of unnecessary money having to be spent to get an agreed and acceptable state of the item with the subcontractor. The moral, then, of these items is that they must be treated as a sub-project of their own and no stone be left unturned to see they are as successful and budget conscious as the main project. Once again, Quality Assurance must be asked to state the procedures, to inspect and test these items as well as they do their own in house items.

QUALITY ASSURANCE CONTINUOUS AUDIT

Last, but not least, the Project Manager must involve the Quality Assurance group in a continuous audit. This Quality Assurance audit process does not, in fact, go on in many companies, and to some extent we have the same old problem of some resentment by the design staffs. While the design staffs can, and do gradually get used to the idea of a Quality Assurance test of their equipment at the end of their design phase, they appear to look suspiciously at the continuous presence of QA staff in the project. However, a quality audit can be exceedingly helpful. It can prevent much wastage of time at the end of the project, putting right what really amount to silly mistakes in terms of quality and reliability by the design engineers, who in this sophisticated and complex technical world must not regard themselves as experts in all things.

As previously mentioned in this book, there can often be disputes between the design engineers and production engineers. The former want to get on with the design, often to a tight timetable, sometimes, unfortunately, almost regardless of cost, and the production engineer wants to have the design suitable for the production processes available, or to be made available. Likewise, quality assurance audit can prevent long test and redesign phases by checking, even if on paper only, the hoped for results of design staff. There will be arguments that this is a repetition of the design work, but this is not so: as this section heading says, it is an audit not a mere repetition of the original work. The definition of 'audit' in respect of, say, financial accounts is the impartial accurate examination of the complete financial picture presented. Quality Assurance Audit is an impartial accurate examination of the complete design picture.

In co-ordinating any job where all or some of the items in Fig. 6.1 apply the Project Manager must use the services of Quality Assurance as much as possible, as they can considerably help him in achieving a trouble free and smooth running project.

Quality Control

This is the important function of carrying out tests, inspection and analysis to ensure that the quality of throughput is as laid down in the quality assurance standards. It involves inspection throughout every part of the product line that the Quality Assurance Quality Control departments have agreed is necessary; patrol inspection and/or at end points of the production line, i.e. key assembly and assembly points and tests of parts or assemblies wholly or partially completed, as well as the whole unit if practicable, and as required by the quality control plan.

In the electronics company we have mentioned previously a fault code sheet was required to be completed for each machine. Figure 6.2 shows this sheet; the numbers against each item are code numbers to enable the statistics of Quality Control to be referenced against faulty items. This sheet is only an example from one company but the amount of detail that can be brought to light is exceedingly beneficial to feed back to manufacturing and design. Only by such work can the various manufacturing stages be brought to adequate efficiency. Of course, this sort of thing can be overdone but usually by a process of patience and logging the truth can be ascertained, faulty manufacture and design remedied and quality checking modified in the light of experience.

The fault code below should be entered in the space provided-overleaf.

Add * to any of the codes if the fault is thought to be due to incorrect design of drawings.

Add # to any of the codes if the fault is thought to be due to lack of instruction or errors in test procedure maintenance schedule, etc.

WIRING	PLANE	CABLEFORM	COMPONENTS	ELECTRONICS	MECHANICAL
O/C-break or not connected	200	300	Component damaged	501	601
Solder joint unsatisfactory	201	301	Component O/C	502	XXX
Wrap joint unsatisfactory	202	302	Component S/C	503	XXX
Crimped joint unsatisfactory	203	303	Incorrect dimension of part	XXX	602
Missing wire	204	304	Incorrect finish or surface		
Shorting in wire or termination	205	305	treatment	XXX	603
Addressing incorrect	206	306	Reason for failure of		
Extra wire or link	207	307	component unknown	504	604
Connector contact unsatisfactory	208	308			
Cause of fault unknown	209	309			

ELECTRONIC ASSEMBLY			MECHANICAL ASSEMBLY INCLUDING COVERS		
Adjustment necessary to clear fault		400	Adjustment necessary to clear fault		700
Component:			Part missing		701
Missing		401	Loose part or fixing device		702
Loose including clamp or fixing		402	Incorrect part fitted including additional parts not required		703
Incorrect item fitted, including additional parts		403	Lubrication unsatisfactory		704
Incorrectly positioned		404	Dirt, dust, oil or foreign substance preventing correct operation		705
Connector contacts making unsatisfactory contact and require cleaning		405	Part incorrectly positioned		706
Insulation faulty		406	Part damaged		707
Short circuit due to foreign material		407	Cause of fault unknown		708
Cause of fault unknown		408			

ELECTRONIC SUB-UNITS FAULTS, e.g. BRICKS, CHASSIS OR POWER SUPPLY			MISCELLANEOUS		
Cause of failure of unit/sub-unit unknown (state brick or unit type number)		100	Test equipment faulty		800
Unit or sub-unit damaged (state brick or unit type number)		101	Fault caused by interference from test equipment		801
Unit or sub-unit missing (state brick or unit type number)		102	Equipment software unsatisfactory		802
			Fault caused by operator error, (may be due to		
			misunderstanding of test procedure)		803
			No code applicable to fault		804

Fig. 6.2 Fault code sheet example

89

STATISTICS IN QUALITY CONTROL

The Project Manager's responsibility may cease with the first production machine if there is to be quantity manufacture of the product. It may, however, go on until the product is completely established. Some knowledge of statistical methods is desirable in order to appreciate what parts of the system require further development or modification if these prove necessary.

There are many excellent volumes on quality control and the statistics employed and we are not going to say too much about this sort of technique here; what is important, however, is an appreciation of the fact of tolerance on all processes and estimations. This is especially necessary in the final tests on the project be it a piece of factory equipment or a task like building a road. The factory equipment will perform to a standard plus or minus a tolerance; this tolerance is determined by many factors, e.g. the intrinsic design including the component tolerances; the temperature; possibly the humidity, manufacturing care and others. A simple example from the southern England electronics manufacturer concerned the tape transport CA314 mentioned in Chapter 4. The speed of the device had to be checked and test result variations were assumed to be part of a symmetrical normal distribution curve such as is illustrated in Fig. 6.3. (Not all process variations can be assumed to fit a normal distribution curve and some curves will not be symmetrical.) Both long and short term speed variations are of vital importance in an industrial magnetic tape transport and correspond to similar effects of wow and flutter in a home entertainment tape recorder.

Dealing with the long term or mean speed condition this is fairly easily checked by tests on each unit revealing the mean speed. If these are tabulated, it will be possible to find out the standard deviation from the mean and from this the chance of further samples being within a range of mean speeds. This is because the relationship between the percentage of chance of finding a given value sample to the standard deviation of a normal curve is fixed. See Fig. 6.3. To find the standard deviation of a normal curve we use the formula

$$\sigma = \sqrt{\left[\frac{\Sigma(x-\bar{x})^2}{n} \right]}$$

where σ = standard deviation.
            x = actual reading, speed variation value, etc.
            $\bar{x}$ = central value (arithmetic mean of all values).
            n = number of readings.

A typical example on the magnetic tape transport might be as follows:

Number of units tested 150
            10 units operating at 70 inches/second
            20 units operating at 69 inches/second
            30 units operating at 68 inches/second
            30 units operating at 71 inches/second
            30 units operating at 72 inches/second
            10 units operating at 73 inches/second
            10 units operating at 67 inches/second
            5 units operating at 66 inches/second
            5 units operating at 74 inches/second

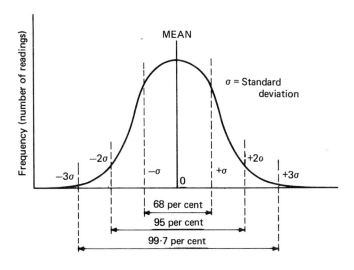

Fig. 6.3 Normal distribution curve

To find the various factors required we can lay out a table, i.e.

Column 1	2	3	4	5	6
x	n	nx	$d = x - \bar{x}$	d^2	nd^2
66	5	330	−4	16	80
67	10	670	−3	9	90
68	30	2040	−2	4	120
69	20	1380	−1	1	20
70	10	700	0	0	0
71	30	2130	+1	1	30
72	30	2160	+2	4	120
73	10	730	+3	9	90
74	5	370	+4	16	80
	150	10,510			630

$\bar{x}$ in column 4 is calculated from:

$$\frac{\text{Total of column 3}}{\text{Total of column 2}} = \frac{10,510}{150} = 70 \cdot 06 \text{ (say } 70 \cdot 00)$$

$$\sigma = \sqrt{\frac{\text{Column 6}}{\text{Column 2}}} = \sqrt{\frac{630}{150}} \simeq 2 \cdot 0 \text{ inches/second-standard deviation}$$

From this and Fig. 6.3 we can see that 68 per cent of readings will be within 70 inches/second $\pm$ 2·0 inches/second; 95 per cent within 70 inches/second $\pm$ 4·0 inches/second; and 99·7 per cent within 70 inches/second $\pm$ 6·0 inches/second. If the specification demands $\pm$ 5 inches/second tolerance then we should have much less than 5 per cent rejection.

There could be a continuous calculation to find the standard deviation, i.e. after every test reading the formula for σ could be reworked. This would be very laborious and instead the Quality Control Department in our case study company set up a control limit chart (Fig. 6.4). The limits are set with reference to the design criteria in that, if we set the limits too wide, we shall not send out sufficiently reliable devices. If the limits are unnecessarily close to the mean we shall get too many warnings or worse still, rejections. There is, thus, a balance which on the one hand causes unnecessary factory rework or adjustment and may eventually raise the unit price, and on the other hand either treats the customer unfairly or

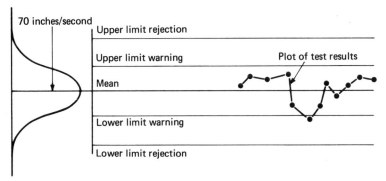

Fig. 6.4 Control limit chart

gets the company a bad name for unreliable equipment. What is certain is that nothing can be perfect, for the company or for the customer, and the job of quality control is to ensure the fine balance referred to above is kept trimmed. It may be, of course, that after investigation design changes are necessary to enable satisfactory balance, and avoid expensive inspection or tests. Once the standard deviation has been calculated, a decision made as to what percentage to pass and what percentage to fail, the control chart will give the necessary warnings for further calculation and perhaps action on design or test.

FACTORY TESTS

The Project Manager will of necessity concern himself more with the major tests of the equipment than with smaller sub-items. This is not to suggest he is concerned only with the former. We know by the very nature of project management this is not so. However, major tests will be of consuming interest because in many ways the Project Manager is the customer's representative all through the project task and major tests are more easily recognizable interfaces as far as the customer is concerned. This is the occasion when the agreed specification can be fully compared with the test results. Of course, in some projects such as road building or the like there is no factory item which can be fully tested before despatch and full test results would comprise traffic analysis and road surface behaviour over a long period.

93

In those cases where the factory unit is possible the key items are:

The agreed specification.

Methods of testing which will allow comparison of the unit under test to the agreed specification.

The test procedures should by this time have all been written in such a manner that the equipment can be checked properly against the specification. In most cases, these checks take place before the customer sees the units in order that any faults can be rectified. The Project Manager must see that in common with all his other work, the above takes place in a highly professional manner as the customer is now appearing and will judge the whole scene.

SITE TESTS

Eventually the equipment, whatever it comprises, will be delivered and whether the delivery is of one unit assembled in the factory or many factory units assembled on site or even made on site, the customer invariably will expect and demand adequate site tests to ensure the whole equipment works to his satisfaction.

Reliability

This is inextricably bound up with quality in the sense that poor quality is almost always going to lead to low reliability. Unnecessarily high quality on the other hand does not always lead to higher reliability; gold plated parts in an intrinsically poor design will not make the part work better and the reliability may be low. We must, therefore, be careful what we mean by quality.

It is rare that a Project Manager does not need to know what the reliability of the product will be. Calculations have to be performed in order that the final reliability can be assessed, because a reliable product most probably saves the customer and/or the company money in smaller maintenance costs. Reliability is usually expressed as a probability, i.e. the probability of a task continuing to be performed adequately for a given period of time. It is axiomatic that the manner of operation and intended purpose must be as initially planned. The usual formula for reliability is

$$R_{(t)} = e^{-t/m} \qquad (6.1)$$

where $R_{(t)}$ is the reliability for a given time (t) and $m =$ the m.t.b.f.

(mean time between failures.) For example, with a guided missile (t) = essentially the flight time of the missile. Therefore, with a reliability of 0·9 (or 90 per cent), 9 out of 10 missiles would successfully hit their target. The background to achieving 90 per cent reliability is more important however. If (m), the m.t.b.f., is expressed in terms of failure rate per 1000 hours (f) then $m = \frac{1}{f}$. Substituting this in eqn. (6.1) above we get,

$$R_{(t)} = e^{-tf} \tag{6.2}$$

In a missile system there will be many component parts each having individual failure rates $f_1, f_2, \ldots, f_n$. The total failure rate $(f) = f_1 + f_2 + \ldots + f_n$ or

$$R_{(t)} = e^{-t(f_1 + f_2 + \ldots + f_n)} = e^{-tf_1} \times e^{-tf_n} \tag{6.3}$$

This can be written to

$$R_{(\text{system})(t)} = R_{1(t)} \times R_{2(t)} \times \ldots \times R_{n(t)} \tag{6.4}$$

This latter statement is the start of all the hard work!

SYSTEM RELIABILITY

System reliability is equal to the product of the reliability of the component parts. While the formulae above provide a theoretical statement on reliability, the answers using these formulae are generally accepted as sufficiently accurate for most working purposes in the light engineering fields. Going back to our missile, suppose there were just two parts with equal reliability; we can easily see that with a system reliability of 0·9, i.e. $R_{s(t)} = 0·9$ each part must be more reliable, i.e. $R_1 R_2 = 0·9$. Therefore, $R_1 = R_2 =$ approximately 0·95. A typical missile system may contain 300,000 parts with varying reliabilities. The individual reliabilities must, therefore, be very high indeed compared to the overall; in the case of the missile system, however, (t) is relatively short, i.e. from firing time to impact.

The above information is a very small introduction to a fascinating subject and there is no shortage of literature on the general theories. The reason, however, for the inclusion of the subject is because more and more accent will be placed on effective reliability of systems in the future due to the increase of 'real time' situations.

REDUNDANCY

What the Project Manager may well have to consider in any system involving a real time situation is that redundancy may have to be built into the system. This redundancy increases the effective reliability of a system to a point where the mean time between breakdowns, statistically speaking, may run into years instead of hours. A real time situation is any activity where we cannot choose to stop and repair anything that stops the whole system because of the impossibility, e.g. aircraft in flight; or the confusion caused, e.g. world wide message switching by the British Post Office.

In these two examples redundancy is built in. In the aircraft case it is much more efficient on, say, four engines than three but it will fly on three. In the message switching example extra equipment is included so that if one lot fails another section can be brought in very quickly and the faulty section repaired while not in use.

In computer systems it is possible to have several computers in operation but the vital parts of the task (the real time tasks) being performed by less than the total number of computers. The extra computers provide 'redundant' standby, either being automatically included in the real time work if the first computer fails, or being switched by the operator if there is time. Real time in this case can mean zero interruption or it can mean that limited short interruptions are feasible. The 'redundant' computers to the real time task can either be truly redundant, i.e. they have no work to do unless the first computer fails or they can perform routine tasks like accounts, payroll statistics, economic studies, etc. which can be interrupted for repair time.

In this sort of computer system the 'effective' reliability can be many years. The expense of such a system is high, of course, compared to a single system.

seven Product Cost

ALL THROUGH THE PROJECT one of the most important tasks for the Project Manager is to know the product cost. A well designed product is worthless if nobody will buy it because it costs too much or, perhaps worse, if the company has contracted to supply at a given cost, to find a substantial loss has been incurred.

There is throughout this book much reference to the words 'product' and 'project'. In 'product cost' we are referring to an end product which is one of a quantity of similar items. In this context, therefore, product and project are not synonymous. The project in this case is the activity comprising design, development and manufacture which enables a quantity of products to be manufactured.

In other cases the project will be the product, e.g. a road, a bridge, a dam, an airfield complex, etc. In costing a project which is also a product we primarily use the budgeting and cost controls presented in other chapters. However, there are still many items within this chapter that will be useful in the project equals product case.

This subject of cost is exceedingly complex although on the surface it looks deceptively simple. The two main problems are multi-project costing and absorption of overheads. In a company making many products it is almost certain that unless the company is purely project orientated with unshared project facilities the costs will be spread over all products by standard overhead costing methods. This may be fair in respect of some of the items, e.g. bought out materials, but can be extremely unfair to a successful project which has to suffer overhead rates from less successful items. Against this,

H

of course, the increases in rates which may arise, even if less successful projects are removed, may considerably alter the apparent benefits of cutting them out. In a large company with a large spread of products the effect of a few unsuccessful products as affecting the costs of the more successful may be quite small. The Project Manager is not likely to be able to alter this state of affairs very easily and must concentrate on his own project with whatever costing methods and rates the company is employing. The Project Manager must, therefore, get his own house in order as detailed below.

Filling the Pot

Work on the 'filling the pot' principle; see Fig. 7.1.

As can be seen from the left hand diagram in Fig. 7.1 the final tolerance, even with 60 per cent of the items not very well known can be much less, in this example ± 19 per cent unknown of the total. As the costing improves with more knowledge of the product, overall tolerance becomes much more acceptable.

In the search for more and more accurate costing the specification

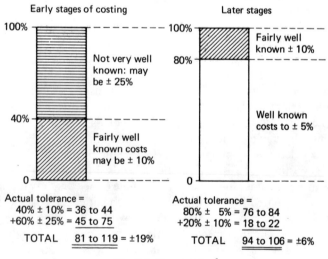

Fig. 7.1 The cost 'pot'

tree becomes increasingly important. We mentioned this in Chapter 5, Fig. 5.5 where the budgets for the project were built up. The product cost tree will be more complex as it extends to every nut, bolt, screw and part in the product or project.

In the case of a new stretch of road it might be appropriate to start the cost breakdown by major items, as Fig. 7.2.

A cost breakdown once started should make its way to every tiny part of the project or product to build a complete cost picture.

The estimating department will want much assistance from designers and others in the early stages of costing as many of the items to be costed are but ideas. A practical approach is to compare if possible the likely result of the idea with some item that has gone before. Is it half the size? Is it as complex? What does it do compared with this or that product? Remembering the 'pot' method, fix a cost and keep modifying afterwards. The worst mistake of all is to delay the collation of an initial cost. As the costing progresses with more inputs from drawings, quotations and other information so the 'pot' will fill and inaccuracies diminish.

Eventually process sheets will be able to appear for some or all of the parts with processes thoroughly costed. Again we must not wait for all of it, but continually update what we have already. At the process sheet stage especially the Project Manager is going to be asked what quantity of the product is going to be sold. This is also an updating necessity as quantity will affect the process in any task. Even in a 'one off' job like a road construction the number of miles and number of bridges will affect the plant requirements and methods of doing the job. With any product likely to be manufactured in large quantities the economies by using the appropriate process can be very significant.

A further consideration for the Project Manager is that costing is an ideal subject for computer assistance. A data bank of continually checked and revised unit costs is very necessary for a multi-project company and enables quick and accurate costing to be established. There is no reason why the data bank cannot include various process method costs for similar tasks so that the cost is appropriate to the quantity to be produced. It is unfortunate that in many product cases the best methods are not used either because the quantities are not accurately known or because the risk of tooling correctly appears too great.

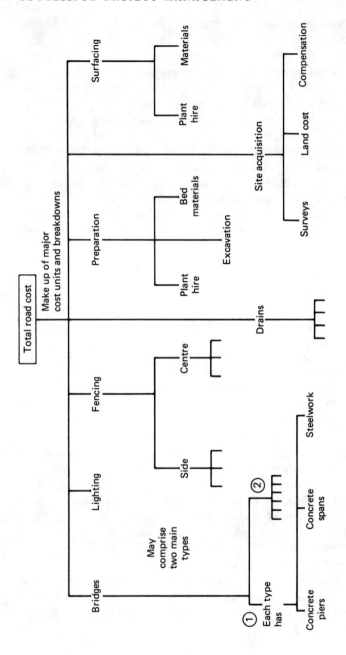

Fig. 7.2 Cost breakdown

This is a problem in setting the cost as minimum capital outlay usually means higher unit costs. The Project Manager should be in the best position to aid the estimators in choosing a minimum risk and lowest unit cost course—coupled with line management acceptance of the processes and tooling costs.

A further very great advantage to rapid cost feedback is by computer aid for the designer. How can an economic design be produced with inadequate knowledge of costs?

Cost Breakdown

In the decision of what cost to give management at the stage when the total tolerances seem large it is essential to adopt a standard approach. Whether the answer is intrinsically correct or not, at least the knowledge of how it was obtained is secure and other costs will follow the same pattern. By feedback from actual results it will be possible to correct the arithmetic processes. For example assume that at an early stage we have a product cost breakdown looking like this:

Unit	1	£10 ± 25 per cent
Unit	2	£15 ± 5 per cent
Unit	3	£100 ± 10 per cent
Unit	4	£300 ± 15 per cent
Unit	5	£400 ± 10 per cent
Unit	6	£600 ± 20 per cent
Unit	7	£1000 ± 5 per cent
Unit	8	£10 ± 50 per cent
Unit	9	£500 ± 5 per cent
Unit	10	£200 ± 20 per cent

Tolerances

What total cost should be passed up to top management? There is a low probability that all tolerances will be high or low together, so some stastistical correction is legitimate. A simple method often used and capable of repetition and checking at a later stage is to take the square root of the mean of the sum of the squares of the tolerances (the root mean square of the tolerances):

Unit	Cost (£)	Tol. % ±	Tolerance	(Tolerance)²
1	10	25	2·5	6·25
2	15	5	0·75	0·56
3	100	10	10	100
4	300	15	45	2025
5	400	10	40	1600
6	600	20	120	14,400
7	1000	5 .	50	2500
8	10	50	5	25
9	500	5	25	625
10	200	20	40	1600
TOTAL	3135	Maximum tolerance	±338·25	22,881·81

$$\text{Mean of sum of squares} = \frac{22,882}{10} = 2288$$

$$\text{and} \sqrt{\frac{\Sigma\,(\text{Tolerance})^2}{n}} = \sqrt{2288} = 47$$

Maximum tolerance of cost = £3135 ± 338
'Statistical correction' gives £3135 ± 47.

If one figure only *has* to be given then bearing in mind the well known law that if things can go wrong they will, it would probably be wise to say £3182 for the complete product of 10 units. All the above relies on the fact that the original costings have been absolutely honest, i.e. that there really is just as much chance of the estimated cost being less as well as more by the tolerance stated. If the tolerances are estimated to be unequal, e.g. −5 per cent + 20 per cent then the statistics will demand more arithmetic!

For those people who remain thoroughly unconvinced that costs can go down as well as up then of course the only solution may be to add the maximum tolerances one way, i.e. + £338 to the mean cost of £3135. The alternative would be to change the mean values of the individual costs!

Cost Accounting

The Project Manager will find it highly desirable to know as much as possible about the cost accounting in his company; even in the best accounting systems there can still be arguments as to how the product should be costed. Take the case of a complex product; it is quite probable that part of the product will be made from product line items, maybe the first such output of those items. Some items, however, may be on the borderline, they may or may not get to be product line. How are these product items to be costed? How much development effort is to be costed on to your product? All of it, or a proportion, because there may be more items from the same development?

These matters affect the Project Manager in so far as he must fight for his project cost to reflect the real costs, whether the information is good or bad news. It is just as incorrect to have cost loadings which do not apply, as understatements. Companies vary considerably in their methods; get to know and understand yours well.

eight Meetings, Communication and Presentation of Information

IN PROJECT MANAGEMENT there will be a maximum of communication because this is the all important oil to lubricate the project's motion towards success. To know the problem is a good portion of the battle won and people knowing is only achieved by maximum communication. Meetings will be necessary because humans are bad at interpretation; we all need clear unambiguous definitions. A lot of these will have to be cleared up at meetings.

Meetings

There are key techniques for meetings as well as project management itself. These are:

There must be an object. Seems common sense doesn't it? You will probably agree with us that a lot of meetings do not seem to have an object; they ramble on. Is there another way of getting the results without a meeting?

The right people must be there. It is no good having a meeting if the people present cannot decide anything. It is not always possible to decide everything at one meeting, but to invite failure by inadequate representation must be avoided.

The meeting must be competent to decide upon the subject. The subject must be within the scope of the meeting level and ability. It is no good for example a meeting of salesmen sitting down to decide what manufacturing process should be carried out to achieve a problem in production, or production engineers trying to decide what percentage sales ought to be in a given area.

Sufficient notice with the *objectives clearly stated on an agenda* must be *sent to the right people* after ensuring *they can be present.* This is really a summary of the items above and refers to the when, what, why, where and who of the meeting.

Now the how– There are broadly speaking four ways a meeting can proceed:

The free for all: no definite results.
The chairman's recital: a monologue not a meeting.
The effective logical, responsive decision making process!
The silent men: no one dares to speak.

We need no prizes to guess the third way is the best and the one we want, but how do we ensure it?

Obviously the chairman can make or break the meeting and provided all the other factors have been attended to then it is 90 per cent up to the chairman whether we get the right results. The next few remarks are thus addressed to chairmen or prospective chairmen.

If you want a meeting have a meeting but don't use it as an excuse to give a lecture to a captive audience.

You will have an agenda because the objectives have already been stated. As far as is sensible stick to the agenda. There is always the chance that an important additional item may arise out of the meeting: be prepared to deal with it.

Do not make silent men by admonishing people if they are slightly irrelevant. Do it gently and lead them back on target. Do not drive them to silence.

There must be no free for all: common courtesies to each other and to the chairman must be the order of the day.

The Agenda

Meetings have to be; there is not yet sufficient communication equipment for everyone to avoid meetings; what should be avoided are long and fruitless meetings. This is where the carefully thought out agenda repays the effort put into it. There are a few basic rules quite apart from the content, which we have stated, must be clear if the objectives are to be achieved. Surprisingly often such commonplace items as time and place are not clearly stated; there may even be obscurity about who is to be present. It is helpful to adopt some standard pattern so that the facts are stated without having to think too much about them, e.g. one could always start with:

A meeting will be held at (PLACE) on

(DATE) at (TIME) to (SUMMARY OF OBJECTIVES)

| To be present | Names and departments |
| | represented |

Note: We say, 'a' meeting. We hope it will be one only!

We say 'meeting', not a rambling discussion or a monologue!

We must know precisely the 'place, 'date' and 'time'

We must have a summary of objectives.

In regard to these latter the objectives should be clearly laid out in the body of the agenda, i.e.

1.0 *Objective No.*

1.1 *Sub-objectives of*

and so on.

A clear agenda will help to get the business done by keeping people to the point.

Minutes

We do not believe in minutes as we usually see them: 'Mr Brown said he thought the matter could be resolved by having a report'. It goes on, 'Mr Smith said he agreed with that'; on and on it goes. 'The chairman asked if there were any dissensions and there were none.'

We believe that if a body of people meet to sort out problems, the notes from the meeting should be, e.g.,

It was agreed equipment A would be manufactured by subcontractor X at the quoted price of £100 to specification 453. Action Mr West, Purchasing Officer.

Obtain within 1 week the cost of the process now proven in No. 2 works.

Action Mr East.

Report to the chairman.

(There could, thus, be a series of actions for different people which could result in reports before or at a further meeting.)

The minutes or notes, therefore, should be *action* notes, not an essay to describe how a number of people spent an afternoon.

There are exceptions to every rule of course; if the meeting took place to prepare a report on some subject for, say, higher management then a report is expected rather than action notes. It is a different kind of meeting. The majority of meetings, however, are more effective in deciding what actions shall take place by agreement and within the competence and authority of the meeting.

Tell It or Write It?

In general communication in and outside the company we know of no substitute for the written statement. There is no need for the 'we beg to remain' type of language but communications, evidence, orders, contracts, statements must all be written. If this sounds a bit like 'trust no-one' this is not the intention. It is our old enemy interpretation again. At least if it is written there is a good chance that questions will arise in due course if the words do not appear to mean what one thought they should mean. How much worse when one comes to the crunch and arguments start about 'you said this or that'. Give the recipient a chance by writing to him. What we have said does not mean that people in close contact and with the subject matter recurring day after day in conversation or meetings have to be all the time writing to one another. Interpretation is almost sure not to be a problem in such circumstances. The clear moral, however, for most people in the majority of cases is, if in doubt, put it in writing. The project is too important, so confirm the important issues covered in discussions.

Communication

In the larger company people have to communicate a great deal. They will, of course, communicate if they want something and know where to get it; what is more difficult is the type of communication by which people are kept informed. This has to happen especially with project management, because there will be constant dangers of cutting across company lines of communication. If this occurs and there is also a lack of communication, friction will result. There is a mixture of annoyance, fright and frustration. Annoyance by being ignored; fright because if it happens too many times the job is eroded; frustration at not being in the centre of the action.

Information Pictures

So far we have defined the task, we have sorted out resources and timescale and have talked a bit about meetings and communication. In regard to the latter there is that old adage that a picture is worth a thousand words. Some pictures follow which help to give information; modifications of these should always be possible to help communications.

In many cases words and lists or tabulations may carry the same information, but the clarity and speed of the information transfer can often be much more effective by pictures. Here is a way that a pictorial presentation can be drawn.

Note that the comparisons in Fig. 8.1 must be in the same mould. It might be misleading to illustrate the number of products, for instance, by a big box and a small box.

Charts

There are many charts of varying type and appearance but they are likely to be based upon a few basic types.

GRAPH OR CURVE

This is perhaps the commonest of all charts and all of us at one time or another have drawn a graph, however simple.

SURFACE CHART

In a similar category is the surface chart. This again is a graph with a continuous line joining the co-ordinate points but this time the surface under the line is filled with line pattern or colour. An impression of size is also gained as well as the movement associated with a graph. Also in the surface type chart comes the cumulative band chart where the surface is divided into several bands, as in Fig. 8.2.

	Company A	Company B
Number of factories = 1	(4 factories)	(3 factories)
Number of men = 1000	15,000	12,000
Number of products = 10	30	20
Number of lost hours through strikes = 500	2000	1250
Capital value of company = £ 20 m	60 m	50 m

Fig. 8.1 Comparison picture

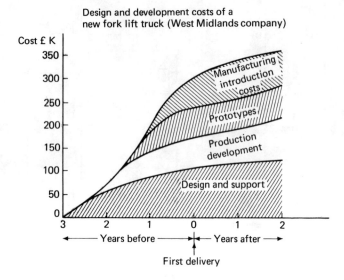

Fig. 8.2 Cumulative strata graph

BAR CHART

There are several versions of this involving comparison bars against targets. The bar chart is showing time of an activity compared against another activity over the same basic time plan, as in Fig. 8.3.

PIE OR CIRCLE CHART

The familiar 'how much slice of cake for this' type of chart, as in Fig. 8.4.

COLUMN

Vertical bars are used to represent a value of one sort or another not necessarily on any time scale, as in Fig. 8.5.

MIXED OR COMBINATION CHARTS

There are many combinations and derivations of the basic chart types that can be drawn up to suit a particular case. An example would be the line of balance chart in Fig. 8.16.

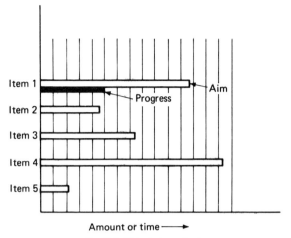

Fig. 8.3 Simple bar chart

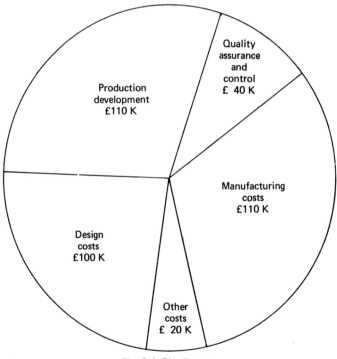

Fig. 8.4 Pie diagram

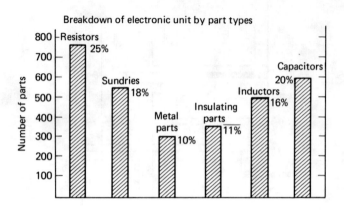

Fig. 8.5 Vertical bar chart

Tables

These appear in a variety of forms, are simple devices and can portray a great deal of information in a small space.

Size → Colour	6·0	6·5	7·0	7·3	7·5	
Green	G6	G65	G7	G73	G75	
Blue	B6	B65	B7	B73	B75	
Red	R6	R65	R7	R73	R75	
Brown	BR6	BR65	BR7	BR73	BR75	

Table of colours and sizes to give buying code for hats

Fig. 8.6 Table 1 example

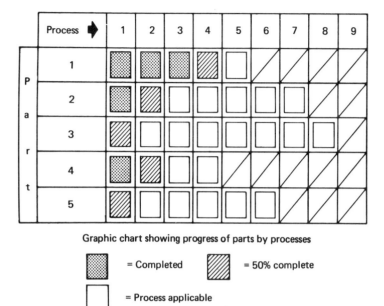

Graphic chart showing progress of parts by processes

= Completed   = 50% complete

= Process applicable

Fig. 8.7 Table 2 example

Management Information

Presentation of information to management and staff at all levels requires much thought, patience and observation by the Project Manager and/or his staff. One of the more important points to remember is that the presentation has to be adjusted to the level of management or staff receiving it. Top management invariably has more than one project or interest to attend to; the information given to them has to be completely self-explanatory. It is unlikely in a new project that the first report will completely succeed in its purpose, but it is essential to find a solution compatible with the needs of top management and the Project Manager. Confidence must be established very quickly that back up information exists in up to the minute form, that line management subscribe to the information where they either can or need to do so; differences must be brought our clearly. The key areas of management information are:

> Costs against budgets at the time.
> Progress against plans at the time.
> Forecasts of costs to be incurred.
> Forecasts of progress completions.
> Problem areas.

These must be clearly presented, but in such a way that inter-relating facts are shown. The whole process is like an advertisement! The facts have to be displayed in order to make a sale easily and quickly.

Time

The project progress in terms of time could be illustrated in the simplest way by comparing key points numbered 1, 2, 3, etc. against actual progress. This could be done in two lines above a date base, the lines marked 'planned' and 'actual'.

Such a simple picture suffers from several disadvantages:

> There is no current forecast of progress against the original plan.
> There is no provision for showing what effort has been expended in the project to date, i.e. the interrelations of cost in money and resources against progress.
> The progress points are not named and a special key would be necessary.
> The back up information reference is not shown.
> A list of dates would have been just as good.

A more comprehensive picture trying to avoid the criticisms above appears in Fig. 8.8 below. It is only one of the many ways as we shall see.

We could just as easily do this in list form instead of quasi-pictorially (Fig. 8.9).

We could add in other information such as cost commitments as distinct from money actually paid out.

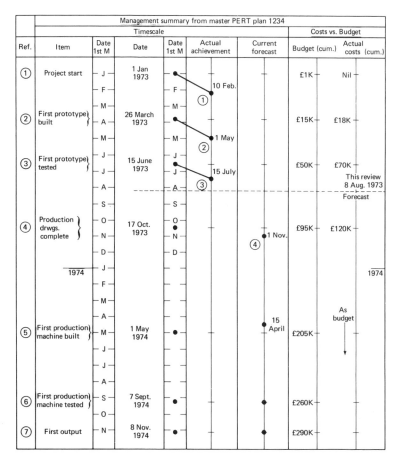

Ref.	Item	\multicolumn{5}{c}{Management summary from master PERT plan 1234}						

		\multicolumn{5}{c}{Timescale}	Costs vs. Budget	
Ref.	Item	Date 1st M	Date	Date 1st M	Actual achievement	Current forecast	Budget (cum.)	Actual costs (cum.)
①	Project start	J	1 Jan 1973	F	● 10 Feb. ①		£1K	Nil
②	First prototype built	A	26 March 1973	M	● 1 May ②		£15K	£18K
③	First prototype tested	J J A	15 June 1973	J J A	15 July ③		£50K	£70K This review 8 Aug. 1973 Forecast
④	Production drwgs. complete	O N D	17 Oct. 1973	O N D	●	● 1 Nov. ④	£95K	£120K
	1974	J F M A						1974
⑤	First production machine built	M	1 May 1974		●	15 April	£205K	As budget
⑥	First production machine tested	S	7 Sept. 1974		●	●	£260K	
⑦	First output	N	8 Nov. 1974		●	●	£290K	

Fig. 8.8 Cost/time summary chart

Costs

A graph form of the costs versus budget together with progress on the task is shown in Fig. 8.10. This is quite comprehensive, and ideal in many ways for a quick management appraisal. It is likely to be acceptable only after confidence is established that all backing information is present and that project progress can be measured accurately enough. This confidence is dependent not only on the integrity and capability of the Project Manager and other staff, but

		Progress			Budget vs. costs		
Number	Item	Planned date	Actual achievement	Current forecast	Budget at planned date	Actual cost	Current forecast
1							
2							
3							
4							

Fig. 8.9 Cost/time summary list

on the definitions attached to key and sub-key progress points. It is not always easy to assess accurately the successful completion of these milestones and some risk inevitably has to be taken. The more detailed the available information, the less must be the risks of the unknown. The integration of time versus costs in Fig. 8.10 can be done in various ways and individual preference plays a large part in what one assumes is the best presentation.

The conclusions one might draw about the results in Fig. 8.10 are several:

Expenditure is over by £38K.
Final expenditure is predicted to be over by £30K.
Dependent upon objective No. 28 the project is well on time.

The action to be taken is:

Detailed reasons must be sought for the overspend, with the project on time it could be underbudgeting.
The predicted overspend must be substantiated, it could be more or less.
A project not in accordance with time or financial budgets must be specially watched until it is right or new targets agreed.

Another type of summary chart appears in Fig. 8.11, this time with the accent on steering a cost and progress course down the centre block. Progress is directly related to the review point. Costs are easily categorized as over- or underspend.

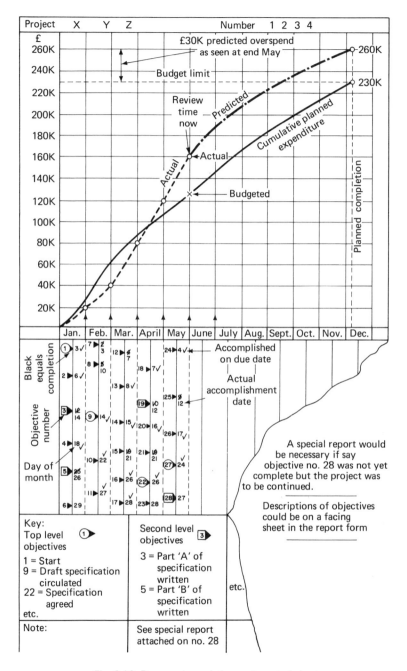

Fig. 8.10 Progress/cumulative cost control sheet

117

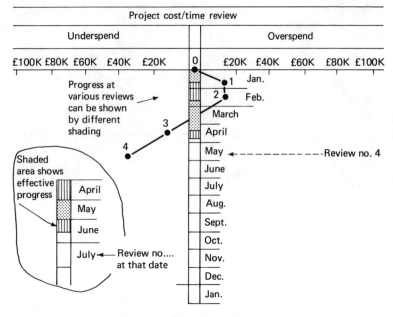

Fig. 8.11 Cost/time review chart

In the example in Fig. 8.11, it can be observed that at review 1 the progress was normal, but there was an overspend occurring. At review 2 the same effect. At review 3 progress was still normal, but an underspend was occurring. At review 4 the underspend was significant and project progress was dragging behind. Like Fig. 8.10, this type of chart is useful, for at a glance views of progress versus costs can be seen, but further details must be sought for the reasons behind such information.

If it is wished Fig. 8.11 can be split so that over- and underspend appear as headings on a cost control chart, with another chart showing the progress behind or in front of the overall planned date or the time at which the chart is presented. The headings by the graphs make this clear.

Moving Averages

In the presentation of information of period figures, say, monthly returns of sales or costs or any similar periodic returns, it is often

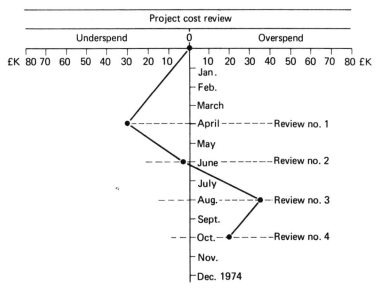

Fig. 8.2 Cost review chart

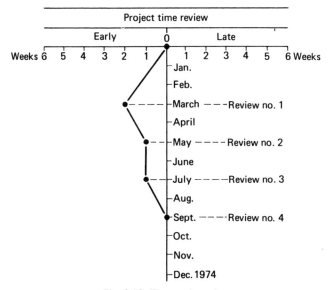

Fig. 8.13 Time review chart

119

desirable to change the fluctuations into a trend curve. Figure 8.15 shows monthly expenditure figures for consumable test materials in a test workshop. Superimposed on this is a 3 monthly moving average curve. It could have just as easily been a 4, 5 or 6 monthly moving average curve if required. The Table shows the construction of the curve.

Such a curve takes out the more violent fluctuations and shows a trend more clearly from which control action can take place.

Line of Balance

Another useful device is the line of balance charting. While this is principally used in manufacturing, as the example will show, it can be used to illustrate other processes.

It is first necessary to know the time order of a process, e.g.

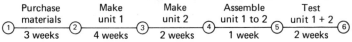

Forecast of project completion date

Reviews	Sept. 1975	Oct.	Nov.	Dec. 1975	Jan.	Feb.	March	April 1976	May	June
1 Full PERT less 'A' division detail 1 – 1 – 74						●				
2 As above inc. 'A' division 1 – 3 – 74									●	
3 After corrections of resource in 'A' division 1 – 5 – 74				●						
4 Full director review meeting 3 – 7 – 74			●							

Planned completion

Fig. 8.14 Completion forecast chart

120

Col. 1	Col. 2	Col. 3	Col. 4	Col. 5	Col. 6
Month	Monthly amounts	3 Months' moving total	3 Months' moving average	6 Months' moving total	6 Months' moving average
JAN.	200	—	—	—	
FEB.	400	—	—	—	
MARCH	300	900	300	—	
APRIL	600	1300	433	—	
MAY	500	1400	466	—	
JUNE	400	1500	500	2400	400
JULY	300	1200	400	2500	416
AUG.	400	1100	366	2500	416
SEPT.	700	1400	466	2900	450
OCT.	600	1700	566	2900	450
NOV.	700	2000	666	3100	516
DEC.	500	1800	600	3200	533

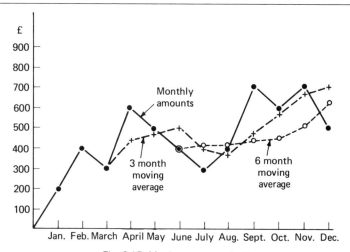

Fig. 8.15 Moving average chart

Secondly the output requirements of the finished product must be known, e.g. the schedule of delivery could be as follows.

		Cum		Cum		Cum
Week	1–10 off	10	11–50 off	420	21–40 off	910
	2–20 off	30	12–50 off	470	22–40 off	950
	3–20 off	50	13–50 off	520	23–40 off	990
	4–30 off	80	14–50 off	570	24–30 off	1020
	5–40 off	120	15–50 off	620	25–30 off	1050
	6–50 off	170	16–50 off	670	26–20 off	1070
	7–50 off	220	17–50 off	720	27–20 off	1090
	8–50 off	270	18–50 off	770	28–20 off	1110
	9–50 off	320	19–50 off	820	29–15 off	1125
	10–50 off	370	20–50 off	870	30–10 off	1135

Thirdly if a review is carried out at, say, week 15 we would expect the state of the units to be as in Fig. 8.16.

We have been rather stressing so far in this chapter the use of simple graphs and charts to give management the information they require. This is only part of the process. Written reports must also be sent. These reports must be very crisp and clear with the triangle of identification concept always in mind. No manager wants to wind his way through a long verbose report only to find the position still not clearly stated at the end. Many words will not substitute for facts, and management require facts in order to be able to help both the company and the report.

From the preparation of concise and informative reports from all the detail available there will be feedbacks and control in the project both by the Project Manager and his management. Key technique 7 —Measure the Project.

In the larger projects serious consideration should be given to the setting up of an operation or information room where the facts of the project can be continually displayed. There is also no technical difficulty of on line to computer links in order that an interactive visual display unit can give the Project Manager up to date information from a project data bank set up for this purpose. The keyboard on the visual display unit will enable interrogation of the data bank by the Project Manager or top management.

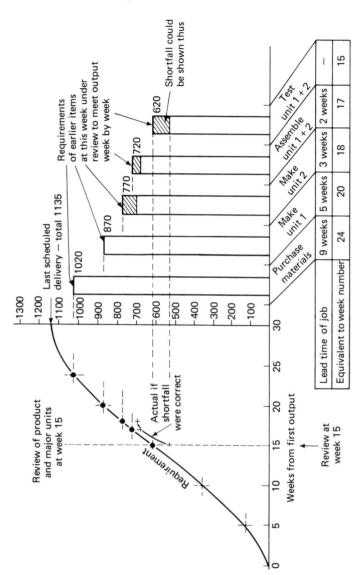

Fig. 8.16 Line of balance chart

nine Project Control

THE WHOLE CONCEPT OF project management is to know, interpret and control the whole project as distinct from any one functional management part, e.g. design, manufacture or testing. The project is viewed continuously as one integrated whole task. This puts a greater responsibility on the Project Manager to report accurately, efficiently, rapidly and clearly upon the project progress. There must be:

> No secrets from top management.
> No lack of planning such that warnings of trouble come too late.
> Dissemination of information adjusted as necessary to all levels of management and staff.
> Progress information in a form acceptable to the recipient.

Equally there must be no excuse for top management:

> In not providing management backing for the project and the Project Manager.
> In not trying to appreciate new ways of information presentation, e.g. PERT, display terminals, etc.

The management information charts we have shown are the balance sheets of situations we find in the project after careful investigation. This sort of searching for the truth in itself provides a control; the searching is primarily done because of reports which have to be rendered regularly or in case of urgency. Such reports will include a selection of the charts in Chapter 8, especially the comprehensive cost and progress chart as Fig. 8.10. A similar type of chart can be produced from a computer PERT time and cost package, but the progress part will vary according to the particular package.

If we now refer back to the project identification triangle, Fig. 4.1, we showed a series of four levels as an example. Rigorous project control consists of checking a series of key events in each level of identification hierarchy. To take a simple example, Fig. 9.1 shows a top level of 5 key events or baselines of a project in the medium to very large category, and two further levels. Each top level key event is completely specified as a major objective or baseline so that no lack of clarity or ambiguity can obscure a positive achievement. To proceed past one of these objectives without it being achieved in all respects may be a decision of the highest management in a company —a board decision or a board sub-committee looking at this particular project. On the other hand the Project Manager may be authorized to make all decisions from the start with the aid of the appropriate company specialist organizations.

Below these top level baselines come the second level; these and other levels will normally always be within the scope of the Project Manager's authority. All events have to be specified in terms of technical progress and cost as originally conceived together with any fresh look in terms of priority, company change decisions, customer change decisions or other influences.

These key events may have hundreds of activities between them and the number of levels of the reporting system is chosen accordingly. The whole concept is to set objectives at varying levels of the task and *manage the project by* assessing the achievement of these *objectives*. The lower level objectives are just as much real links in the chain, and all too often are ignored.

Identification of Objectives (General)

We have already stated that these must be fully specified so that we are clearly aware whether we have met the objectives. There is no doubt this is the critical area of control. Each objective has two main areas:

> FINANCIAL Product cost and project cost at the objective point. These are synonymous only in the the one off project.

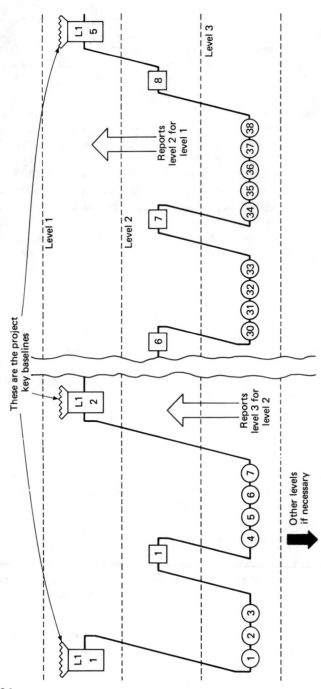

Fig. 9.1 Objectives and key levels chart

126

PROGRESS In technical terms. This may be exceedingly difficult in research area objectives, though simple in technical process areas where tests can establish the position.

Each can be influenced by new factors. Ignoring these, however, we are left with problems in each category.

In the financial area we cannot accept on its own merit a statement of underspend, on target or overspend. Take underspend first: this may not be serious, the budget may have been too high. How are we to judge? Against progress? Is the project behind schedule? If it is, then underspend may be the reason, the resources may not have been deployed correctly. On the other hand, there may be technical difficulties which really demanded an overspend as the correct solution, i.e. get more resources into the task. The extra cost may be small weighed against, say, penalties for being late.

With overspend, similar remarks apply. The overspend may or may not be serious. It has to be weighed against progress and the original budget. Even being exactly on course with spending may have any of the pitfalls of over- or underspend.

To sum up facets cannot be isolated, they must be weighed against each other and any additional control information that can be brought to bear.

PROGRESS This can be even more difficult because unlike money it cannot always be counted in units. If one of our objectives in the lower level of key events hierarchy is measured against its specification on the due date and fails for some reason, is the whole programme to be stopped while we wait for the objective to be fully achieved? Probably not, but we take a risk immediately if we proceed. A decision has to be made; will this deficiency slow up the project now or later? Will it stop the project later? Rules and specifications like budgets can be ignored at times but we must know, record and watch with even more attention the subsequent progress to see if our decision was right. To blunder past key events with impunity is project suicide.

OTHER CONSIDERATIONS As each key event time occurs (or before if it is at all possible) we must be aware whether there are:

Company changes in priority, budgets or specification.
Customer changes.
Other changes, e.g. changes in the law, finance acts, etc.

Will these affect the key event we are examining? This is not so frightening as it looks because the third item will rarely apply, and we are very likely to know about the first two in a progressive manner as the job proceeds.

Progress Reporting

To aid the procedure of reporting, some standard input form is necessary. Figure 9.2 is only an example, the exact form is not important, but a disciplined flow of progress reporting is essential.

For the top level objectives, an adaptation of Fig. 8.14 can be used to show the estimated progress of each objective on the same sheet. Reasons for any variation from the planned time should be stated against the objective (Fig. 9.3).

Cost Analysis and Control

In the make up of project costs, derived from the addition of all the packages of work or sub-jobs that make up the total, the costs will vary according to the resources put in to them. That sounds very simple and obvious but there is a third effect—time.

If a task costs £100 per week with 2 men involved and the 'normal' time is 10 weeks duration the cost is clearly £1000. If we now want to cut the time to 8 weeks it is certain the cost will go up beyond the £1000. This is because extra men, overtime or mechanical aids will be involved. In addition there will be a minimum time for the task no matter what extra money is spent.

Conversely, if the time exceeds the 10 weeks the cost may not fall below the additional cost of £100 per week.

These two simple truisms of project costs produce the general project cost curve of Fig. 9.4.

Project . . . .   Project number . . . .

PROGRESS SUMMARY REPORT

Date . . . .   Period . . . . to . . . . . .

PROGRESS

   Write in here achievements against schedule especially
the key events of all levels. Refer to tests or other
proofs of event specification being fully met. Be
particularly careful in the case of top level baselines.

PROBLEMS

   Write here succinct accounts of technical or other problems
which could now, or in the future, cause lack of progress.
Deal especially with the major issues.

FUTURE PLANS

   Write here what are your forecasts of progress and costs.
Plans for dealing with existing problems.

REFERENCE TO ACCOMPANYING DOCUMENTS

   Refer to key event achievement proofs: cost progress charts,
and other information to show PRECISELY the project
position. (Various charts in line with the examples we have
covered would be included in this section; Chapters 8 and 9.)

Department or division . . . .   Compiled by . . . .

Project Manager . . . .

                  Sheet of sheets

Fig. 9.2 Progress summary report

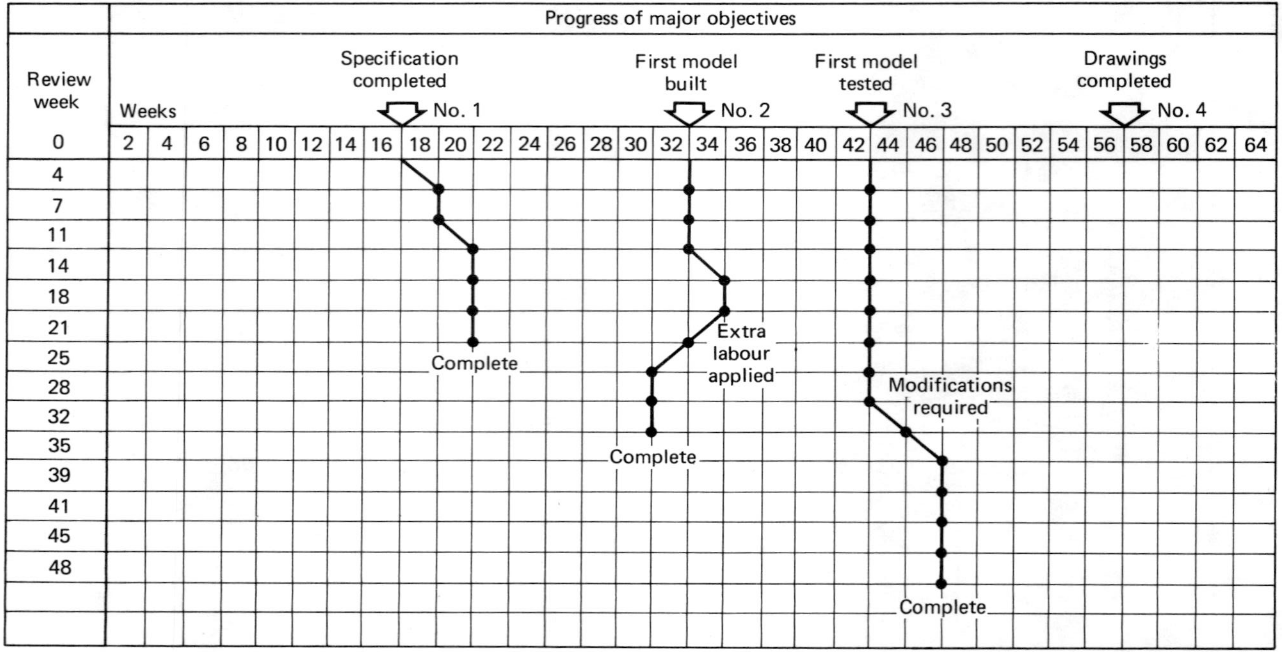

Fig. 9.3 Major objectives progress chart

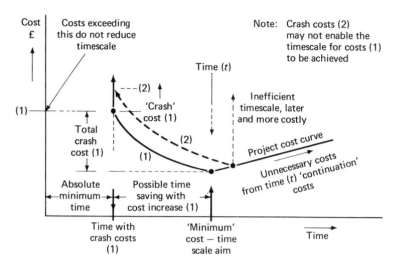

Fig. 9.4 General project cost curve

While the qualitative picture is simple to envisage it is not usually so easy to put figures on the picture and draw the correct curve for a particular project. If, however, we are to control the costs properly, we must try and find out as much as possible about them and their relationship to the time scale. We require the information for four reasons:

In the initial timing and costing of the project we need to know what timescale we can achieve for £x costs. It may not be possible to achieve it at all for £x!

Given a certain timescale what will the cost be?

If the project is running late, how much will it cost to bring it back on time, if indeed it can be done at all.

If the project time scale has to be shortened, even though the project is on time, the crash cost/time relationship must be known.

The costs of all activities on the project network must be known to satisfy the first two requirements of the four above, including additional costs, both 'crash' and 'late' costs. In respect to lateness and crash action we need to know more about the critical and near critical path items. This can be done manually in a very small project,

131

but computer assistance in our opinion is essential over about 100 activities to perform full cost and resource analysis. The two are obviously very much interlinked.

Construction of a Project Cost Curve

To do this we need to know the 'normal' costs, the 'continuation' costs and the 'crash' costs on the network critical and near critical paths.

Figure 9.5 has entered on it the 'normal' times (in weeks) in order to establish the base for the next steps. The first table sets down the 'normal' costs and cost of reducing the time scale.

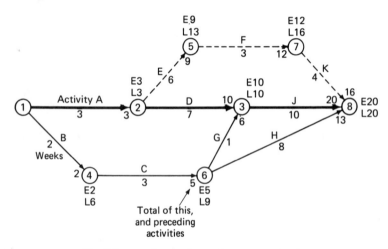

Fig. 9.5 PERT diagram for cost curve construction

These costs have to be found by obtaining alternative estimates for the different cost approaches for each activity.

Examining now only the critical path of Fig. 9.5 activities A, D and J have the following cost characteristics (from Fig. 9.6).

Plotting these on Fig. 9.7 we obtain the appropriate project cost curve. In this example, the limits on the critical path items did not cause an encroachment into the next critical path, i.e. E—F—K.

132

Activity	'Normal' duration	'Normal' cost (£)	'Continuation' costs per week (£)	Crash costs For 'minimum' time		For 'stated' time	
				Time	£	Time	£
A	3	300	100	2	820	$2\frac{1}{2}$	500
B	2	300	150	1	600	$1\frac{1}{2}$	500
C	3	600	200	2	900	$2\frac{1}{2}$	730
D	7	700	100	6	980	$6\frac{1}{2}$	800
E	6	300	50	4	450	5	375
F	3	150	50	2	250	$2\frac{1}{2}$	200
G	1	150	150	$\frac{1}{2}$	250	$\frac{3}{4}$	200
H	8	160	20	6	250	7	200
J	1ɔ	1000	100	8	1540	9	1130
K	4	1200	300	2	2100	3	1600
Total cost		4860					

Fig. 9.6 Costs table

Event 8, if we suffered the extra crash costs, is now at week 16 instead of 20. This is equal to E—F—K. If the reduction in time on the original critical path could have brought event 8 below 16 weeks, then activities E, F and K would have to be examined to see if they could be reduced.

A further point in looking at time reduction on the critical path is, where significant differences exist in the increases in costs per week saved, the lower cost items should be adjusted first to decrease the slope of the crash cost curve, i.e. make c/t a minimum.

Penalties and Crash Costs

If a project is running late and penalties are likely, then some simple arithmetic with the project cost curve and the penalty build up will enable the most economic solution to be found.

133

| Activity | Crash cost/time | | | | Continuation costs per week |
| | Stated | | Minimum | | |
	Time saved	Cost	Time saved	Cost	
A	$\frac{1}{2}$	200	1	520	100
D	$\frac{1}{2}$	100	1	280	100
J	1	130	2	540	100

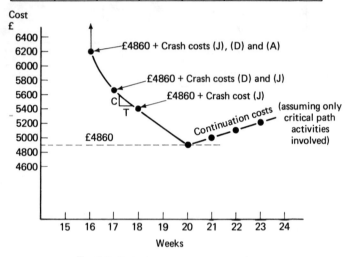

Fig. 9.7 Project cost curve construction

We will assume the project is running 4 weeks late; the penalties are £5000 per week for late delivery; crash costs have the form according to Fig. 9.8; and the budget will be spent at the original planned date. From Fig. 9.8 it can be seen that an acceptance of 2 weeks' penalties would be the cheapest solution rather than incur any more crash costs.

Moral: Try not to be late!

Losing the 'least' amount of money is highly unsatisfactory!

Making Decisions, especially Technical Ones

The art of decision making or, we would prefer, the science of decision making, is obviously going to be affected very much by a

Planned completion	Project cost line	Penalties (cumulative)	Crash cost extra expense	Total
Budget	£233,000	Nil	£80,000	£313,000
1 week late	£243,000	£5000	£45,000	£293,000
2 weeks late	£253,000	£10,000	£8000	£271,000
3 weeks late	£263,000	£15,000	£3000	£281,000
4 weeks late	£273,000	£20,000	Nil	£293,000

Fig. 9.8 Crash costs table

particular industry and its needs. How does the Project Manager manage technical decisions? It is almost certain the Project Manager cannot be an expert in all skills involved, though he will, however, know the language. There will be other managers or staff with specialist skills. Do we just believe what they say? Without doubt we must rely on the man we place, or who has been placed in the particular skill area to make decisions on problems involving that skill unless, and until, we assess that he is not capable enough. What else can we do? It depends on whether the decision is part of a top level, second level or lower level key objective. It may be felt by the Project Manager that in some of the highest decisions other specialist opinions must be sought. There is nothing wrong in this, and it is not a question of mistrust of the man in your project. If the issue is large enough there is never any excuse for not seeking all the technical opinion you feel necessary, until the issue is as clearcut as you believe it is likely to become or should be. The overriding responsibility is to the project success; if any of the staff and management cannot agree that premise, they may require education or replacing!

The first thing to do when starting to make the decision is to apply key technique 1—Define the Objective. What is the real decision we have to make? It may not be that which we first thought! One technical decision which one of us was asked to make was which of two bought out power supplies should be purchased. There were pros and cons for each make. After questioning the Purchasing Manager, the Design Engineer and the Production Manager, it was found that this was not really the right question. What should have been asked was should we buy out or make inside. Everyone had assumed we had to buy this particular unit. When the question was looked at in depth, it was found we could make them ourselves at an acceptable cost. After the definition then came the analysis of resources, key technique 2 and so on. We had found a more acceptable alternative solution.

In general it is essential to have more than one solution for a problem. Judgement can then be applied. How do we judge the problem in general terms?

Why not the bookmaker approach? Put a judgement on the chance of success of doing it at all. Try and put science to work: put a probability on each action. We know this will not solve the problem on its own. There may also have to be an experience pattern to back the first judgement, but why not make the first decision in the light of full information of all kinds.

What about resources? It may be easy to make a decision involving half the company, but apart from unpopularity, impossibility or sheer non-necessity could the problem be licked another way, costing little? On the other hand if the answer to the problem needs large resources then the Project Manager must say so and convince management accordingly.

Is the answer to the problem needed urgently? It may be that the answer can consist of a chipping away, with the minimum of risk but taking time. It may be, however, that fast action is really needed. If it is, get the company running first. It is easier to make it run in the right direction than try and push it over.

You will have noticed that key techniques 1, 2 and 3 are still the base of the decision making process. Once the decision is made we can move on.

The Project Manager, above all things, must not believe he is an expert in all the skills; for a production engineering problem get the best production engineers around you and the same for all other skills. The further we advance into this technological age, the more complex the projects; the shorter the time scales, then the ideal combination is project management organization and techniques, coupled with the best specialist skills.

Changes

The progress of the project will be marked by achievements of objectives; in any company today there will also be a set of manufacturing drawings produced as the progress of the project allows. These drawings and accompanying information are committing the company to a way of manufacture and manufactured items. It is vital that the Project Manager exercises firm control with the help of Quality Assurance and project engineers over:

The production engineering:

Is the product correctly tooled.

Is the correct plant used.

Are the right processes used, etc. for the quantities of the product, as these affect the manufacturing drawings.

The state of the drawings:

In terms of standards.

In reflecting the correct state of the design.

The change control over the drawings:

Of changes due to production engineering.

Of changes due to technical changes:

In the design stage.

In manufacturing.

In customer use.

Changes cost money; wrong drawings cost money; wrong processes cost money; so everything costs money! The real point at issue, however, is that:

The drawings must be as correct as possible in the first place. (There is a little story about this. In a company we know the manager was used to issuing a series of instructions to his staff. The last instruction was numbered 15. His next instruction to all staff was, 'There will be no further mistakes on drawings. There have been too many and I will not tolerate any more.' His instruction was numbered 15!)

There will, however, be changes continually produced and we must have a control procedure to filter them.

Change Control

To ensure that change control is effective, a change control centre is imperative. The centre can be simple, i.e. vested in one person in a suitable department to make sure that changes are controlled, or on the other hand a whole department may have to be involved.

Unless changes are firmly controlled (not suppressed), the project will almost certainly be late and more costly.

How are changes controlled? Well it sounds easy. Once a project baseline or key objective is passed there should be the utmost resistance to change affecting that baseline. However, like all simple rules, when you get down to the earthy job of running a project, it does not seem so easy as reading about it! It can be done though!

In the south of England electronics company we have mentioned previously, a firm change control system operates with two classes of change:

Class I changes are generally considered to be essential and affect baselines. Because of the believed essential nature of these changes there is all the more reason for a very thorough vetting of them with a cost and time penalty firmly assessed. Class I changes invariably affect:

Specified function.
Performance.
Maintainability.
Reliability.
System interfaces and perhaps other equipment.

Class II changes are desirable but not essential. They could include items such as colour of paint not quite correct; internal metalwork not to drawing but tolerable; cables too long, etc.

There is an engineering change control department which, while the project is at the prototype development stage, receives copies of changes raised by the engineers. There is no action by the ECCD until agreement is reached with reference to the project plan and actual progress that the prototype development has been concluded and that manufacturing drawings sufficient for Quality Assurance tests and examinations are to be issued or a present issue of drawing stated to be such.

The next phase is twofold. Quality Assurance is testing and examining the prototype and changes will be produced as a result of their work. Production engineers will be continuing to modify methods of manufacture until the last permitted time and changes will again be produced. At this stage the Change Control Department exercises a light rein over the changes, watching especially those changes that might affect the function of the equipment. Quality Assurance will also be joining in the vetting to ensure their testing of the prototype is not being undermined by the proposed changes.

Once the prototype has passed the product approval tests the control by ECCD tightens considerably. Manufacturing drawings, especially detail parts, are being released for production and preparation of the larger more costly assembly drawings is being carried out. Tooling is proceeding and the cost per change is rising. All changes are now rigorously examined and have to pay their way. The balance sheet of some changes is very difficult to prepare. The balance of, say, easier serviceability in a given area, against £x manufacturing cost is not straightforward. The important point is that a machinery does exist to weigh the advantages and disadvantages of making a change in a non-emotive fashion.

The usual procedure for changes is firstly a change request with which the ECCD can approach interested parties, e.g. Designer, Drawing Office, Production Engineer and Quality Assurance and obtain a considered opinion on the merit or otherwise in financial, operational, maintainability, etc. terms. ECCD must then decide if the change shall proceed. If the change request is approved, then ECCD will ask the originator to put forward a formal change proposal with, this time, full details of the change and its effect in drawing change details or other changes such as specifications.

The whole point of a formal change procedure is not to stop necessary changes but to eliminate unnecessary ones and, above all, to give to management the knowledge of the cost, advantages and disadvantages of change actions.

part three More about
Project Management

ten Subcontractors

Why Subcontract?

At some stage in nearly every project, it will be necessary to consider putting some work out to subcontract. This may be clear right from the start or it may become clear as the planning of the project proceeds.

The subject of subcontractors is sometimes an emotive one. At the one extreme are those who grudge the profit made by a subcontractor, and who believe that all work should be done 'in house' to secure all the profit available in the project to themselves. At the other extreme are those Project Managers, generally in large firms, who want to contract out as much as possible. They see the price of special items calculated with contingency piled on contingency and with heavy mark ups added for company overheads. In some such cases a small item may cost £500, when if subcontracted or bought out, it could be obtained for £50.

Whether or not to employ subcontractors must be decided on the basis of the facts in each case. The criterion by which to judge is basically that of profit. Will there be more profit or less on the project if subcontractors are used? Can the resources available be used on this or another company project to greater profit if some work is contracted out? Can the project be undertaken at all if there are no subcontractors? Can the firm maintain a higher level of morale among its staff, if work not of a continuing nature is contracted out?

In selecting the subcontractor, the first essential is not the lowest price. It is, can the subcontractor do the job? Has he the specialist knowledge and skill? Has he the necessary plant or equipment? So far as possible this should be established before a firm is even invited to tender.

The next stage is to determine whether the firm is a solid one likely to remain in business. If a subcontractor goes out of business, when a major project is well under way, the cost can be far greater than the price of the subcontract.

It is only after these points have been established that weight should be given to the best price and delivery quoted. A high price and long delivery in the case of a substantial subcontract may indicate that the tenderer does not particularly want the job and is not prepared to make any special effort to get it. On the other hand it may be an indication that he has studied it carefully and fully appreciates the difficulties and complexities of the job. This draws attention to an essential prerequisite to the selection and control of subcontractors. You must know what you want them to do. Stated like that it seems laughably obvious. Yet it is surprising how often subcontracts are placed on the basis of vague ideas of what may be possible. Such subcontracts are more appropriate to research and development than to normal projects.

To obtain sound tenders it is necessary to have given a clear description of what is required. At the same time the Project Manager should establish what the work is worth and how the price should be built up. This gives him a criterion against which to judge tenders. Thereafter discussions with a tenderer should soon show whether the quotation of a low price and quick delivery are due to special competence and new ideas or whether they are due to lack of comprehension.

You may well ask, if it is necessary to do all this work, why not go on and do the work 'in house'. It will surely cut out all the time and trouble taken over preparing an invitation to tender and in evaluating tenders.

One answer to this is that it is one thing to know what is required and in outline how it is done. It is something entirely different to have the resources to be able to do the work. The other answer is that if you undertake a large number of similar but not identical projects, you may have contacts with specialist firms who regularly sub-contract to you on a single tender basis. This is particularly common in the construction and computer industries.

Reasons which may lead you to subcontract include the following:

To obtain special items, of which you only require a few, but which specialist firms make in large numbers.

To obtain access to special knowledge and skills.

Great care must be exercised when giving subcontracts for this reason. Requirements have to be specified in such a way that they are absolutely clear and unambiguous. At the same time you must avoid going into unnecessary detail about method. This will cramp the subcontractor's style and may increase his costs and lead to a less satisfactory result than if he were left to apply his expertise to the problem. Changes to the specified requirements will inevitably lead to either delay or increased price or more probably both.

In considering placing subcontracts for this reason think carefully about how long you will require the specialist knowledge and skills. Can you dispense with them when the work is completed or must you have some continuing provision for maintenance? Consider a large computer user, who contracts out the writing of a suite of programs. Such programs invariably contain 'bugs' at the time the programs are handed over. Some of these 'bugs' quickly become apparent. Others may not appear for months or years till some unforeseen coincidence of events occurs. Can 'in house' programmers maintain the programs right from the start of live running or will they need some backing? Almost certainly support will be needed from the manufacturer or software house for several months at least.

In overseas projects or in development areas to provide some work and profit for local people, hence hopefully generating some local goodwill. In some overseas projects the main contract may only be awarded on the basis that certain work is locally subcontracted.

To augment the resources of your firm, in a period when they would otherwise be overloaded. This may be because your firm has been caught out in its planning and cannot acquire the resources itself in time to apply them to this project. Alternatively it may be a

144

matter of policy to maintain staff and equipment at a level where they can be continuously employed. The peaks are then handled by subcontract. This helps to maintain a steady work force and avoids the problems that come from having underemployed resources.

Controlling Subcontractors

Once the decision to go out to subcontract has been made and the subcontractors have been selected, the problems of control come to the foreground. Problems of control fall into two areas, the commercial and practical.

COMMERCIAL

Basically, the commercial problem is to ensure that the contract covers the needs of the situation. If the project is being handled by a main contractor, then his subcontracts must be commercially in line with the main contract. If they are not, he can be subjected to an unpleasant squeeze. Even if the control of the project is in house and not the subject of a main contract, it is necessary to ensure that the progress of the project is not endangered by any default of subcontractors.

The commercial points will be covered in the contract with the subcontractor. The following points must be considered:

> Price.
> Requirements of contract.
> Delivery.
> Maintenance.
> Quality and acceptance tests.
> Guarantees.
> Insurance and liabilities.
> Penalties.

The firm's contract department or solicitor will draw up the contracts and will cover the fine legal points. The Project Manager's job is to ensure that the facts to be covered in the contract are clear.

PRICE

In considering the price in the contract remember the time value of money. In one large project in the electronics industry, the main contractor found that he eventually paid £50,000 more than he had bargained for on a £1 million contract. He let the terms in his own contract with the customer get out of line with the subcontract terms. As a result the contract with the subcontractor provided for progress payments, whereas the main contract did not. The main contractor then had the problem of finding the money before he was due to be paid. Fortunately the main contractor was a large company and able to raise the money. However, the cost in interest payments of making progress payments was £50,000 and that bit nastily into the profits on the whole contract. Price seems straightforward enough. However, in overseas projects the price may be expressed in a foreign currency, in which case there should be provision for the effects of changes in currency exchange rates. It may also be necessary to specify the place of payment and if this is overseas to consider how the payment will be affected by currency transfer regulations. It may be necessary to buy foreign currency forward to meet the contract commitments or it may be desirable to insure against currency risks.

REQUIREMENTS OF CONTRACT

The requirements covered by the price must be crystal clear. We have already seen the need for a clear specification for the job. Now it is necessary to look at the items peripheral to the main job. If the subcontract is for special equipment, does the price cover test equipment and initial stock of spares? Does the price cover the provision of manuals and if so how many copies? If the equipment is to be linked with other equipment, where will this take place and what are the arrangements for technical support during linking and testing? If the project will be completed overseas for an overseas customer, does the price cover visits by the subcontractor's staff to the site for discussion and installation?

In fact the project must be thought right through to the end and all the requirements to be placed on the subcontractor must be identified and covered in the contract. Even if all the items can not be specified, it must be clear what is covered by the price. There must also be agreement on how extras will be priced.

DELIVERY

The delivery date must be in accord with the PERT chart for the project and the place of delivery must also be stated. Delivery may be to customer site, to one of your firm's factories or may take place on the subcontractor's premises. In any case the time involved in packing, shipping, linking to other equipment and testing with it must not be overlooked.

MAINTENANCE

Provision must be made for maintenance in the contract. If the subcontractor is to do the maintenance, what will be the basis? Will he provide a resident engineer? Or will maintenance be on call? If on call what response time is involved? Is he required to have test equipment and spares on site? If not, and there are national frontiers between the site and the base spares, what will be the effect of transportation and customs delays?

If the subcontractor is not to do the maintenance, then the matter cannot just be forgotten. Who will do the maintenance? What will be their requirement for training, test equipment, spares, instruction manuals? How far must these be supplied by the subcontractor? A point to be borne in mind here is that some firms price their products so that the price of the initial delivery is cut to the bone. Their profits are made on supplying extensions to the original equipment and spare parts at a high price.

QUALITY

The quality of the work done by subcontractors is of prime concern to the Project Manager. The success of the whole project depends upon it. So does his own reputation and that of his firm. So far as the final customer is concerned, the project is being executed by the main contractor. He is not interested in excuses about poor performance by subcontractors. The quality of the work must, therefore, be specified and carefully checked against specification.

GUARANTEES

The smooth running of the project once it 'goes live' will depend upon continued good performance of all the component parts of the installation including those supplied or built by subcontractors. While the acceptance tests will be aimed at ensuring that the finished work will be fit for its purpose, some guarantee of performance may be desirable. This is particularly important if the final customer demands performances guarantees in his contract. Such guarantees may cover performance in the sense of error rates; mean time between faults; average length of time the whole or part of an installation will be out of service due to break down in a day, week, month or longer period; acceptable tolerances on measurements or performance; and a great many more.

One trap to watch for here is the cumulative effect of poor performance in one part of a system on the performance of the whole. The cumulative effect of errors through the system must be calculated with care. This is best done by starting with the stated performance of the individual pieces of equipment in the chain and working out the worst case. This can then be checked with the project (or customer) requirements. What is absolutely essential is that this must be done before agreeing that a given performance can be given to the final user.

There may be some special risks involved in a project arising from technical considerations, which a legal or commercial man may not spot for himself. The Project Manager should highlight these. He must also ensure that any specific requirements he may have for control of the subcontractor are included.

Penalties

There is one last sad aspect of the subcontractor's contract which must be considered. This is the question of penalties. Should a penalty for non-performance of the contract be included? If so, what should the penalty be? Should it be linked to a cancellation clause?

In a sense a penalty clause is a limitation of the liability of the supplier. On the other hand if a penalty clause exists, payment of the penalty can be secured more quickly and certainly than if damages have to be pursued in the courts without the support of a penalty clause.

Where a subcontractor depends on your firm for a high proportion of his business a penalty clause may be unnecessary. Reducing the flow of business to him is a far more effective sanction.

Where a project is time critical—and most projects are—a penalty clause may be desirable as a spur to performance. The subcontractor is selling his services to you. His salesman may be one of those who believes in getting the orders—and his bonus—first and worrying about how his firm will execute the order later. In such a case a demand for a stiff penalty clause at least ensures that his seniors in the firm will look carefully at whether the conditions of the contract can be performed. If the penalty is too small the subcontractor may prefer to pay rather than incur crash costs involved in bringing his work back on schedule.

In the early stages of a project all concerned tend to be in optimistic mood and to regard the actual payment of penalties as unlikely and discussion of the possibility as academic. But the possibility is always there: 'The best laid plans of mice and men . . .'. The penalties placed on subcontractors should line up with those of the main contractor.

A computer manufacturer tendered for a turnkey project worth about £1,200,000. Included in the tender was equipment to be developed by a subcontractor and priced at £450,000. The final user held out for a penalty clause, giving him a penalty of $\frac{1}{2}$ per cent of the price for each week of delay in the handover date up to a maximum of 15 per cent. The subcontractor was only prepared to accept his own 'standard' penalty clause, giving $\frac{1}{4}$ per cent a week up to a maximum penalty of 5 per cent. Finally after a lot of hard negotiating the main penalty was brought down to the maximum of 10 per cent while the subcontractor agreed to accept a penalty of $7\frac{1}{2}$ per cent. The project was important to the main contractor. It was a key step to establishing himself in a potentially large overseas market. The contract was signed and the project went ahead. At one stage in the life of the project things started to go wrong and a realistic look was taken at the penalty situation. Suppose the project was complete on time except for the subcontractor's equipment, which was 20 weeks late. The penalty would be £120,000 on the main contract of which only £15,000 could be recovered from the subcontractor. This was because the subcontractor's penalty did not relate to the value of the whole project but only to the price of his contribution. Furthermore the 'price' in this case was not the final price of £450,000. It was the 'price' which the subcontractor had quoted to the main contractor, i.e. £300,000. In other words the penalty was on £300,000 not on £450,000. Although the subcontractor had accepted a maximum penalty of $7\frac{1}{2}$ per cent, he had retained the weekly penalty rate of $\frac{1}{4}$ per cent which meant that the main contractor suffered the maximum penalties at 10 per cent, while the subcontractor was restricted to 5 per cent—only two thirds of his maximum.

This tale had a happy ending because all pressure was put on the subcontractor once the cost of failure was established. Delivery was made on time and no penalties were paid. It does, however, suggest some points worth considering when establishing penalties in project subcontracts.

With all this talk of penalties, do not overlook the fact that you make your money from completing the project successfully on time —not from penalties extracted from defaulting subcontractors.

We have gone on at length about all the contract points to watch with subcontractors. These are important. Remember, however, there must in the end be something in it for the subcontractor. He is in business to earn a living and make a profit. If he is tied down to an unprofitable contract, he may look for every opportunity to default or to economize on the specification. If you force a subcontractor into bankruptcy, you and your project may suffer more than he does. The moral is that subcontractors should be treated fairly and given a fair contract, which will allow them to make a reasonable profit. In these conditions they are most likely to give of their best.

Practical

The first thing to consider is how far you need to exercise practical control of the subcontractor. Is it sufficient on the one hand to rely completely on the subcontractor to deliver at the agreed time and place? Is it sufficient merely to monitor his progress against a previously agreed timetable? Must there be full involvement in the progress of the work and constant adjustment to the plans for the project both as a result of the progress of this subcontractor and as a result of the progress of the project as a whole?

The answer to these questions depends both on the nature of the work subcontracted and the nature of the project. The overall PERT chart for the project should be examined to see whether the work of this subcontractor lies on or near the critical path of the project.

Where a subcontractor is supplying standard equipment from his normal range well in advance of the date it is needed for the project, it may be sufficient to await the arrival of the item. However, even in this case, it is worth a regular check that the delivery date can still be met. A supplier, left to himself, may not bother to warn you of delay or slippage until close to the original delivery date. The mere fact that you telephone or write should set off a routine enquiry within the subcontractor's organization. It may alert him to slippage. It should certainly give you early warning to bring pressure to bear or make alternative arrangements.

For most subcontractors a regular system of control is needed. This will vary according to circumstances, but can probably be built up as a variation around the following. The subcontractor should be required to produce a timetable detailing the main milestones. For a large or complex subcontract this should be in the form of a PERT network. Regular progress meetings should then be held and the subcontractor should report progress against the PERT chart. Although interest will, of course, be concentrated on critical path events and activities, the report should also confirm that other activities due for completion have in fact been completed—or if not a new completion date should be given. Where a serious deviation from the plan either due to slippage or because of a change of requirements has been accepted then a revised PERT will be required.

The number of people attending the progress meeting should be as small as possible—ideally only one person from each side, and the meetings should be kept as short as possible. See Chapter 8 on this point.

As well as progress meetings it will be necessary to have regular technical meetings to solve problems which arise in the course of the work. Where the subcontract is for equipment to be developed it may be desirable to have a quality engineer or inspector permanently in the subcontractor's works. On a construction site, a clerk of works will carry out constant physical checking of the standard of work done, before it is concealed by subsequent work.

Computer Projects

One of the most difficult types of subcontract to control is one for computer software. These contracts are too often approached in a rush without proper planning and consideration. A completion date and price is set and both are normally wildly exceeded. All parties feel cheated or misjudged.

This is how one computer manufacturer set about controlling a particular software subcontract. The whole project was worth over £2 million. It included work on special software and applications programs, which was subcontracted to a software house for over £½ million. The project was undertaken for a customer on a turnkey basis. The timescale was tight—2 years from start to finish and it was anticipated that the customer's requirements would change over the period.

It was clear from the start that only a very tight control would prevent the project from turning into a shambles. The Project Manager had a Software Manager to help him with the control of the software part of the project. The first 3 months were taken up with reaching agreement on the specification and setting up the control mechanism. When the specifications were agreed, master copies were made, identified and held by each of the customer, main contractor and subcontractor. The specifications were accompanied by a note of points, which it was agreed had still to be resolved. These specifications were the basis of the contract. The price and time scale were confirmed as applying to these specifications. Thereafter if any of the three parties required a change to the specification they submitted a written request for specification change. The implications were considered. The subcontractor produced an estimate of the effect on delivery and the amount of programmer time and computer time required. The price of the changes was obtained by a simple agreed formula. A specification committee, consisting of representatives of the three parties concerned, then met to consider the alteration to the specification. Formal minutes of these meetings were kept. Where an alteration to the specification was agreed a numbered specification amendment was issued. This system worked well though there were disagreements from time to time when the estimates proved faulty. However, the estimates improved as the project progressed and all parties also learned to interpret them. Even with this strict control of the basic specification, goodwill and trust between the parties were essential. Disagreements could, however, be discussed cooly against a background of carefully documented fact. Incidentally in a contract of this kind it is essential for the pricing of the original contract and the subsequent amendments to be on the same basis, i.e. fixed price or a cost plus formula. This is because of the interaction between the work on the original specifications and the work on subsequent amendments.

In par
diagram w
whole 2 years
as linked progr
much shorter. In
chart for 3 months a
PERT diagram. Each acti
estimated to take about a f

Each month the software pr
of the manufacturer's Project Ma
the subcontractor's Project Manage
formal written report of progress again
and discussed. Ways in which the two pa
over the problems were explored. The o
always reviewed with care. The meetings lasted
took place alternately on the contractor's an
premises. After the meeting all four went off to lunc
relaxed conversation over a drink and lunch helped to
relations and also enabled the Project Manager to obtain in
informally which might not otherwise have been forthcom
certain critical points in the project the meetings took place
frequently than once a month. In addition the Software Manag
was in touch daily with the subcontractor's Progress Manager. The
subcontractor also made available a small office on his premises for
the Software Manager. The project Software Manager had the right
to see all team progress reports and trial plans, results and reports.

At the end of the project there was a variation in both price and
delivery against the original plans. It was, however, a controlled
variation. All parties knew why it had taken place. It had not crept
up and taken them unawares. All parties were satisfied that they had
had a fair deal and that the project had been executed efficiently and
economically.

Successful Subcontracting

When employing subcontractors, select those whom you can trust to
do a good job. Specify your requirements clearly. Document carefully any variation in your requirements and its effects on the project.
Control your subcontractors effectively, but allow them to make a
fair profit; leave something in it for them.

allel with the work on the specificat...
as produced as a sub-set of the project PERT. (
it was made up of broad activities. Some of these such
am testing lasted several months—others were
ddition there was a much more detailed PERT
head, which slotted into the broad software
ity on this was a programmer's task, usually
ortnight.
ogress committee met. This consisted
nager, the Software Manager, plus
r and his Progress Manager. A
st the PERT diagram was made
ries could help each other
erall delivery date was
about 2 hours. They
d subcontractor's
h together. The
ustain good
ormation
ing. At
nore
er

r
a
d
d.

to

the

must

..... what PERT is, how worthwhile it is for project management
and what is involved in using it.

The most useful result of PERT without doubt is the analytic and
critical approach it brings to bear on a project being examined for
the first time; this initial review of a project by PERT is probably the
most used and useful attribute. There are millions of people performing tasks great and small and of high and low complexity. Many
of these tasks will succeed without PERT; some may fail even with
PERT, but in the business and technological world the keynote is
always to get the dice loaded in favour of success. This means that
every artifice or technique that can be brought to bear economically
should be brought to bear. For time planning and simple resource

154

planning, PERT is an excellent practical device. For cost planning and more elaborate resource planning PERT is even more useful, but probably requires a greater understanding to fully succeed in presenting information in a digestible form.

PERT as a Technique

In project management we stress all the time the need to plan, to maintain and control the plan, and modify the plan, if we have to, in a controlled manner. There is no doubt, and it would be surprising if it were otherwise, that a large number of project activities gives rise to a considerable physical and mental problem in keeping track of each activity and its progress. The real problem is interaction; it is a rare occasion that the progress of one activity does not affect many others.

Gantt charts or bar charts show job layout by time and progress thereof and are exceedingly useful tools. What they cannot show is the continuing interrelationship of these jobs, especially when they change in timescale and resources, unless only a very few activities are involved. In even small sized projects of perhaps 100 activities the interrelationship can be complex. PERT is a tidy tool, or at least it forces the user to be tidy; an isolated activity cannot exist, since it has to be preceded and succeeded by others (except, of course, the first and last activities). This is the first great advantage; as the mind plans out the job, so the flow diagram evolves, and even begins to remind the user of gaps in the drawing. If you have not 'PERT'ed' before, try the simple example in Fig. 11.3. The major activities in the construction of a garden shed are listed in Fig. 11.1. Figure 11.2 shows what a bar chart might look like and Fig. 11.3 the PERT diagram. (Please don't write and argue with the way we build our garden sheds!) You will easily see the principles and, we believe, quickly recognize that the discipline of flow diagram working, for that is really what PERT is, helps greatly to avoid missing out key linking activities. However, even in this simple example many of the pitfalls that project progress can suffer are beginning to show themselves.

TIMESCALE

Without questioning the individual times in this example, is the timescale the shortest that can be achieved? In other words, we

Item number	Item or activity	Activity time (hours)
1	Clear site	10
2	Dig topsoil away	5
3	Obtain hardcore	20
4	Lay hardcore foundation	5
5	Obtain ballast	15
6	Obtain cement	15
7	Mix concrete	8
8	Lay concrete	3
9	Obtain bolts	5
10	Set bolts in concrete for attaching wood structure	2
11	Obtain timber	25
12	Make sides of shed	3
13	Make back of shed	3
14	Make front of shed	4
15	Make roof of shed	3
16	Make door of shed	3
17	Obtain windows	30
18	Fit windows	3
19	Obtain glass to size	10
20	Obtain putty	5
21	Fit glass into windows	3
22	Obtain timber preservative	5
23	Paint all timber with preservative	3
24	Fit sides, front and back together on bolts in concrete	6
25	Fit roof	3
26	Fit door	3
	also required to have been done:	
27	Decide to build shed	
28	Decide where to build	30
29	Decide what to build	
30	Draw or sketch shed for quantity of parts assessment and construction details	

Fig. 11.1 List of activities for garden shed construction

Activity time (working hours)

Number	Item or activity	Activity individual times
1	Clear site	10
2	Dig topsoil away	5
3	Obtain hardcore	20
4	Lay hardcore foundation	5
5	Obtain ballast	15
6	Obtain cement	15
7	Mix concrete	8
8	Lay concrete	3
9	Obtain bolts	5
10	Set bolts in concrete for attaching wood structure	2
11	Obtain timber	25
12	Make sides of shed	3
13	Make back of shed	3
14	Make front of shed	4
15	Make roof of shed	3
16	Make door of shed	3
17	Obtain windows	30
18	Fit windows	3
19	Obtain glass to size	10
20	Obtain putty	5
21	Fit glass into windows	3
22	Obtain timber preservative	5
23	Paint all timber with preservative	3
24	Fit sides, front and back together on bolts in concrete	6
25	Fit roof	3
26	Fit door	3

Fig. 11.2 Bar chart of activities

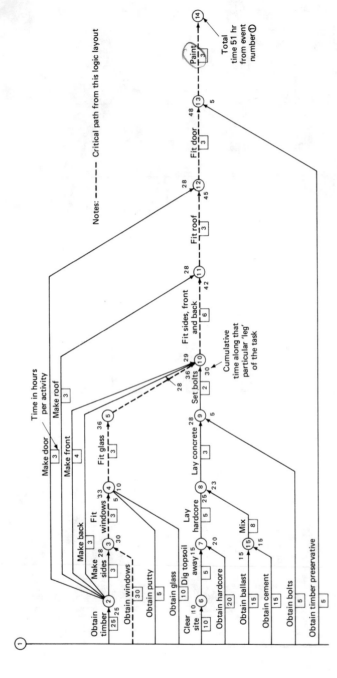

Fig. 11.3 PERT chart of activities

158

question the logic of the contruction. Looking at Fig. 11.3 we can see where the critical path runs. Can we rearrange the logic to achieve a shorter path? For example:

Could we put the preservative paint on the shed sections beforehand, rather than right at the end. This would possibly cut 3 hours activity 13 – 14 down to NIL or maybe $\frac{1}{2}$ hour for final touching up.

Could we fit the door in the sides before final assembly, which might cut another 3 hours out.

The critical path runs up through fitting windows and glass. Could we do this later, i.e. take activity 5 – 10 and move it to become 5 – 11 . This would help a lot.

COSTS

Again, leaving aside a cheaper form of construction, it should be noticed that, although in this instance there may be nothing of great value, it would be a different story if the bolts cost £1000 each. We take only 5 hours to get them, according to the bar chart, and then leave them waiting in our stores for many hours before use. The same with the timber preservative. Without running risks, materials should be ordered to arrive when required and not a long time before.

Timescale is important regarding costs, because in general there is an optimum timescale for every job. In this example, if men of various skills were employed, it would be costly to keep them hanging around while other skills were being used, e.g. if someone were making the roof, they would in theory wait at event number 11 in Fig. 11.3 for 14 hours until the roof could be fitted. In practice, of course, on this sort of job one man might do the lot but, on a large project, this sort of waste can easily occur.

RESOURCES

As just stated, one man might have to do all the work on this shed. If so, our tacit assumption that activities 2 – 10 , and 2 – 11 , and 2 – 12 could go on at the same time would be wrong. These activities would have to be in series, instead of parallel.

It is clear that a technical knowledge of the particular subject must exist or that co-ordination of this knowledge take place. In this case the job is a simple one and the list has co-ordinated the knowledge to prepare a diagram.

PERT then is certainly not a gimmick (there are still people who think it is); it is an exceedingly valuable tool, well proven in many industries. Very rarely is there any argument that its initial use in a project really sorts out what often is a complex maze of activity linking. As a technique PERT has other advantages:

It enables the user to see clearly those activities which are critical to success in terms of time; those where some delay is acceptable either in lower resources applied, or a delayed start. If delays are experienced on a particular activity, the effects can be seen almost immediately because of the activity linking.

Many methods of presenting information have been evolved, i.e. earliest or latest start dates or finish dates; allowable delays; critical path activities; activities in allowable delay order, etc. These aid the Project Manager or user to see quickly the project position.

PERT as a technique seems clearly to be a great advantage to a lot of firms and a lot of people, and we feel strongly that it is a logical, intensely useful tool for project management. What then goes wrong sometimes in the use of PERT? Why is it sometimes not appreciated by management? To find out the answers to these questions, we must start with an examination of the basic PERT.

Disadvantages

The Logic of the Plan

In a very simple project there is no difficulty in ascertaining the correct logic to use, and indeed there might be some advantage where an autocratic approach could be taken, and the minimum of consultation carried out! However, this would only be safe where the 'autocrat' knew about all the aspects that he had calculated in the logic. In any company, this situation is theoretical and many people will in fact be involved. In a medium to large company, there is bound to be a breakdown of the organization into various groups or departments, and in general it is safe to say that the original flow of the PERT diagram, representing the work in the project, touches almost all of the departments. It is often found that even the main logic flow is not clear, i.e. do we always go from Department A to

Depatment B and to Department C, or do we sometimes go via Department C to Department B. With several departments, this in itself would be bad enough, but we are likely to find in a practical project PERT diagram that not only is there a primary departmental logic problem, but there are likely to be several levels of breakdown below the department. There is, therefore, a great likelihood of difficulty in finding a route for the activities which is:

Accepted by all departments.
Applicable to this project in particular.

In fact, it is often the case that the first example of PERT usage in a company on a largish project reveals for the first time that, surprising as it may seem, the path of work through the company is not clear, has never been clear and requires a fair amount of work to get clear.

Time and Resource Estimation

Let us suppose that after many false starts, and this is the usual experience, a PERT chart is finally produced showing the logic of the work flow and that, in general, the various managers of the departments have subscribed to the logic. We now have to test the logic in terms of detailed activity times, and this is where the fun and games begin. There is an initial suspicion that having to give times to the activities on a particular project may reveal too much of the department's sweet running inefficiency. However, putting aside these suspicions which certainly can affect the working of any type of system such as PERT, we are left with genuine difficulties that beset the individuals who have the somewhat onerous job of estimating time and resources in a particular project. To the contributor some of the difficulties may appear thus:

Has the job been specified sufficiently?
On even a reasonable specification basis, has management given a clear indication of what the resources of the department will be when this project comes to fruition? Should resources, present or future, be taken into consideration at all?
Has the type of work that this project demands been done before, and if not is there sufficient information on the subject to enable sensible estimates to be made?

Should the contributor answer all the questions demanded; should he go to other colleagues; will their estimate be better than his?

What if the estimates are wrong, can they be changed; should some hidden contingency be added? Will there be trouble if estimates prove wrong?

What notice should be taken of what other departments have said?

How can we overcome the difficulties of the contributor? Firstly the Project Manager must see that the task is understood as thoroughly as is possible at that time.

Encouragement must be given to contributors to seek out the truth themselves, to identify themselves with the project and assist in defining the tasks. Contributors must search both inside and outside the company for relevant information from which to prepare the best possible estimates.

The Project Manager must not make the mistake of obtaining information from the wrong person. That sounds too obvious to have to be stated, but it can well be that the real information on a particular part of a project activity lies with person A rather than person B, and that the former does not happen to be in the limelight on that particular occasion. The basic data for the activity information must be sought out extremely carefully, cross checking where necessary so that the maximum experience can be obtained to bear on the information.

What of the resources? It obviously does make a difference whether a senior or junior is put to work on the actual job when it comes. Indeed, is it one or many people to be employed? In general, the contributor at the lower level should ignore resources availability as far as possible. He should state that it would take, say, 6 weeks to do a particular job and that he has allowed certain resources to do the job. As the PERT plan goes up the management tree the awareness of resources and the likelihood of what resources will be available will increase, and a balancing process will take place. This will first be done in conjunction with the original contributor who can state his case in detail. Contributors must have confidence in themselves and their management. Project Managers must help to give them backing in times of stress so that the contributors do not feel inhibited from estimating and correcting estimates if it is necessary to do so.

One of the more difficult functions of a Project Manager is to assess whether the changes in progress success should have been anticipated and what personnel he can rely on for accurate estimates and assessments.

Contingencies

This subject is both a blessing on occasions and a curse on others. There is really only one golden rule, however. Individual contributors, after assessing a task by whatever process suits them best, should not add contingencies. They must be prepared to defend in a professional manner their estimates to management. The latter in their wisdom may add contingencies provided they are at a high enough level of the network, e.g. if 10 activities comprise a department total job then any contingency should only be added by the Departmental Manager and shown to be such. In addition, of course, the manager may disagree with the individual activities and adjust them up or down, but not include deliberately an extra time as pure contingency.

The moral then should be clear. Let the best estimates by the qualified people be subjected to proper management investigation; adjust the results if necessary; only add contingency in clear and visible lumps at reasonably high levels of the network.

Why have we said all this? If contingency is not treated in this way, it runs rife and project overall times become so obviously long that the whole PERT system goes into disrepute. If contingencies are clearly shown top management can leave or chop out as they decide. That is one of the things they are paid for.

Other Departments

Contributors should only take notice of what other departments are saying on the PERT chart in so far as the information directly affects the contributor. It is fatal when a contributor is unduly influenced against a chosen estimate just because Department X says 'It always takes 6 weeks', or 'It can't be done in 3 months' etc. The Project Manager, having succeeded in getting information from reliable sources, must not use it until he has cleared it with the management hierarchy. If he does not do this, some part of the management chain in all probability will not underwrite the information and this will make life very difficult for all. Quite apart from such a difficulty, the Project Manager has to realize that the management chain is there for a purpose. We stress this point to the limit of, perhaps, underlining the obvious, but throughout much practical experience lack of underwriting by the management chain can be the rock upon which a likely looking PERT system can founder.

Education

Going back to the question of gathering the basic data, it can be seen that there will be a problem for the Project Manager in that:

> He would not have the personal time to go deeply into each department, e.g. to find the right sources of information.
>
> He would immediately run the risk of annoying the management chain at that particular point by interfering in their local departmental affairs.

There must then be, coupled with all the mechanics of the PERT system in the information gathering and underwriting, an education process for personnel and the management chain on the parts they have to play in providing information to a PERT system. Inevitably, a large part of this education process will fall to the Project Manager to perform, simply because he is at the interface with these people. If he is the right person, he will be much more effective than instructions passed down through the company administrative chain. One of the more difficult parts of the education process will be to encourage individuals in the ranks of the information giving process to make sure that they too have consulted their colleagues as necessary, especially where the activity or process has not been done before, in order that the best estimate of time and resources can be given. This will also involve the study of any relevant periodicals, papers, seminars, etc. to ensure that the fullest information on the subject is gathered. If one now looks at the whole process of information gathering for planning purposes, whether one is using PERT or not, it can be seen that the whole structure is only as sound as the foundations, the foundations in this particular case being hundreds, perhaps thousands, of detailed pieces of information. What we have said is, of course, no more than key technique 1, i.e. define the task thoroughly and then the remaining key techniques can be proceeded with.

To illustrate in a simple manner the foundations principle, Fig. 11.4 shows how a summary network is supported by more detail in a sub-network, in turn supported by a further sub-network. Often the detail networks are termed frag nets. It should be noted that the detail networks can either be a continuous breakdown of activities from the summary network or perhaps related to departmental breakdown. For example in Fig. 11.4 the activities 1 to 7 and 7 to 8 on the summary network might be one department's responsibility while 1 to 2, etc. may be that of another department.

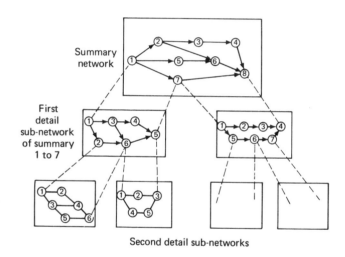

Fig. 11.4 Summary and sub-networks

Behind Closed Doors!

In a fairly well established company, there will be a tendency for some departments to say, indeed as they may have always done, 'It will be all right on the day'. They cannot give details for this particular job, but they get through the work as it comes. The problem in these cases is to prove that what is said may not be true. The problem, as

165

we shall see illustrated later, is that with the many parallel paths in a PERT network, and obviously before PERT came along there were still the same parallel paths in the work operations, there is always room for slippage which can go unnoticed. Other activities have been late and, therefore, enabled other departments to claim they are not late. This means that in most cases there is a high probability of an increase in productivity because of the thorough examination needed to fill in the PERT network. As a first project is done and more information comes to light on the relationship between the initial PERT network logic and activity times against the modifications that had to occur to it, a picture will build up of those areas which can be improved. There is, of course, a danger in applying these principles too rigidly. If one, for example, does not allow some controlled flexibility in those parts of the parallel paths which do not need to operate fully stretched, the result will be that departments work with increased staffs, overtime, etc. unnecessarily, and project costs will rise above the most economic level.

Updating

As the project proceeds there are bound to be changes in both the logic and progress of activities, different to that originally conceived. This does not necessarily mean that anything is wrong as key technique 7 states that planning must be a continuous process. In the seeking of the original information for activity times and resources, much effort was employed to make sure that the information was good. The updating of the network is really the second test for the contributors. They must now honestly appraise their progress and state categorically how far along the planned path they have actually proceeded. If the activity time was 20 weeks, 8 weeks have elapsed and re-examination of the activity reveals that 14 further weeks of work are required, then it is vital that this information comes to light. When one imagines that a PERT plan can contain from, say, 100 activities up to many thousands, then the accumulation of 'white lies', honest wrong beliefs and any incompetence in revealing progress information can completely wreck the project, let alone the contribution PERT can make.

One of the problems about updating is that some of the initial enthusiasm in drawing up the logic for the first time, in sorting out some apparent management and company problems, however minor they may be, may have waned, and the updating seems to be a somewhat unnecessary labour. This is the moment when the Project Manager must prove his worth by sticking to the correct course of action and demanding an efficient updating process regularly from all contributors.

The physical work required in displaying the results of the updating vary very much. In a small project of a hundred activities, it is quite simple to recalculate the total activity time, the critical path and various float figures by hand and have them typed out within an hour or two. With the larger number of activities, say from 300 upwards, the work begins to increase and will demand assistance for the Project Manager if he is carrying out his other functions of technical control in a proper manner. In the higher ranges of activities of 300 upwards then the use of a computer becomes necessary, not just for the amount of work it can do, but for the short time it can do it in. It would be possible to do it by hand with sufficient labour, but there would obviously be marginal returns after, perhaps, two or three people were involved and to complete the job would probably take too long to make the updating exercise valuable in its own right. Updating invariably implies new information availability, and if it is not done quickly, then the value of the exercise is lost. The above is not meant to imply that the smaller PERT systems cannot also usefully be updated by the help of a computer. Hand operation should be avoided wherever possible, as the computer can not only do the work fast and accurately, but can provide a very varied set of output information. This is important in order that top management shall be briefed in a manner that is not only up to date, but suits their particular way of looking at the progress results.

twelve Value for Money

What is Value?

'Value may be defined as the relationship between function and cost. In all cases value is greatest when the cost of obtaining a required function or service, at a particular time and place with the essential qualities, is at a minimum.'

This is a definition from a value analysis manual by the British Productivity Council, and it goes on to qualify this.

> 'Everything that needs to be known to contribute to better value is contained in the above statement provided that:
> 1 We have a product or process that functions.
> 2 The product or process can be made available where and when the customer requires it.
> 3 There is a demand for the product or process.
> 4 The product or process functions to the customer's satisfaction and to the customer's specified degree of reliability.
> 5 The product or process meets the customer's requirement with regard to eye-appeal, prestige of possession, and exchange value.
> 6 From the manufacturer's viewpoint, the process or product meets all these requirements at the lowest possible cost, and is a profitable venture.'

We will take a deeper look at the value question, but before we do it is useful to list some of the items appearing in the minds of cost conscious individuals.

168

Cost Consciousness

There are few businessmen, or people responsible for budgets however small, who would admit to not being cost conscious. Lack of cost consciousness, however, is an insiduous happening. The best of us drop our guard on occasions and our money, or our company's, is spent unnecessarily. Now, to be penny wise and pound foolish is not what cost consciousness is about. Pence do matter whether they were 'old' pence or 'new' pence, and so do pounds. What matters more, however, in the long run is an understanding of exactly what we do when extra costs are incurred because of our inefficiency or our failure to watch out for the 'spending bug'. Equally, of course, we may often incur waste because we do not spend money.

In any organization large or small there is waste; in the big companies the waste is often both large and recognizable. In the smaller companies the amounts may be smaller, but proportionate to the capital employed may be the same or worse than the large company. Waste occurs in many ways:

A market is suddenly lost or the demand slackens very considerably. Materials and plant are now excessive. Even with rapid management action much money may have to be written off over the short or long term.
Overstaffing has grown up in the company.
Staff supervision is slack.
Overstocking of materials or work in progress is occurring.
Budget control is slack.
Expenses and consumable items are not sufficiently controlled.
Product costs are too high either because of poor design, insufficient production engineering or inefficient manufacture.
Tooling and plant is insufficient and labour costs rise.
Working conditions are poor and output is consequently low.
In not generally looking for *value*.

Many of these items or derivatives of them are not problems the Project Manager can solve directly on his particular project. He can, however, play a very important part in helping to optimize value which, as we shall see, can and usually does result in a direct increase in the company profits.

Key technique 5 Know the cost.
Key technique 6 Optimize the value.

These two key techniques are complementary and are weapons project management can use. Both are heightened in effectiveness by the use of value engineering and value analysis.

It is generally accepted that value engineering is the operation of optimizing value at the engineering or development stage of a project, whereas value analysis is optimizing the value when items are in the manufacturing stage. Dependent upon the type and quantity of a product so the emphasis can be placed upon either or both value engineering or analysis.

What is absolutely certain is that value engineering or value analysis will either reduce costs, leaving the same or better quality and function, or it will improve quality and function while leaving the costs the same. It is generally accepted that prices are much more dictated by the market place than by the product cost. By definition, then, lower costs mean higher profits if the product quality and function remain acceptable.

There are also very worthwhile fall outs from value exercises; costing, purchasing, engineering, production engineering and other areas can learn and improve from the experience.

Value Analysis

We will start with value analysis because in many ways it is easier not only to appreciate, but also to prove. We have looked into value analysis at more than a dozen companies and have been actively engaged in our own company on the subject. It can be said, quite categorically:

Have faith. Start up value analysis properly; give it a fair chance. It will reward you with figures of 5 to 15 per cent reduction in costs, after expenses, sometimes much greater, without lowering quality or reliability and probably improving them.

Some firms claim higher figures for overall savings; we know 5 to 10 per cent is achievable and is the more typical experience. We say above have faith; an act of faith certainly is required to start any new department that costs money, but this is one cost which positively will be repaid.

We say, start up value analysis properly and give it a chance. What has to be done is to get proper advice and there are several consultant firms who can help if necessary. Give it a chance because it may take a year to become really effective and feed back results available to underwrite the decision to employ the techniques.

What is the best way to start up value analysis? There are several methods:

> Let consultants come in to organize it.
> Choose a man whom the company believes can start it up and let him get on with it.
> Hire a man whom the company believes can do it and let him get on with it.

Which way is the best? It depends absolutely on what sort of a company you are. While, for example, one company we know did not go to consultants there was no particular reason for this decision. The company slowly started into value analysis after a seminar by the British Productivity Council which, in common with most of the BPC seminars, was exceedingly helpful and professionally carried out. If you can afford it, consultants are probably the best method and will give you a flying start. If you cannot afford consultants coming in to the company, you must still afford value analysis and a BPC seminar would certainly be a good start for your chosen man or men, as well as a course or two with consultants on their own premises, which is much cheaper than their coming to you.

What sort of man should be chosen? We list a number of features, but have deliberately stopped short of a very full description as the company structure does have some bearing on the final job specification and hence man specification.

Firstly, it is essential to possess the full faith that value analysis will succeed; to be able to communicate this faith to others with sincerity and conviction, but with tact and understanding, and the ability to listen, analyse and combat such old beliefs as 'we've tried it before'.

171

Secondly, to be able to co-ordinate and enthuse others in the actual value analysis processes. This implies a thorough study by the value co-ordinator into value analysis techniques and their practical operation.

Thirdly, be aware of the arch enemy always round the corner—The I am right and why can't you see it attitude, egotistical thinking. The implementation of value analysis is going to involve new ways of thinking for all concerned, and patience, understanding and much education are needed.

Finally, of course, to be educated sufficiently in the general sense and trained sufficiently in the particular field of work that is being operated upon.

More than this description must be left to individual managements to provide. What else must management do to make sure of success?

Your value co-ordinator must not be left entirely on his own. You have chosen him for his various abilities, including co-ordination, but remember he is not the General Manager. You must support his work by seeing that line management back his efforts.

Value Analysis Techniques

Value analysis and cost reduction programmes are often confused. The two are very different and one does not stop the other. Cost reduction is usually performing a given function at a lower cost by altering the materials or methods.

The central theme of value analysis is to question at all times the function of the equipment and every part within it. This involves a series of set questions each to be pursued in depth. They are:

Is the equipment (or part) necessary at all?

Note that this includes the complete equipment downwards into the component parts. If you wonder at the inclusion of the complete equipment, perhaps the costing examination will reveal that some equipments may be selling at a loss! More often, of course, the equipment as a whole is accepted. The investigation refers to all parts within it.

Is the equipment (or part) function being performed at the lowest cost consistent with the quality and reliability requirements?

Note that this can also mean higher quality and/or reliability achieved at the same cost.

To obtain the answers to the above, thus permitting a more profitable solution, involves two major areas:

A series of procedure disciplines to be carried out.
The 'forcing' of ideas from specialists which will provide the basis for more profitable solutions.

Dealing with the latter first, we have found that a satisfactory way to promote the necessary ideas is by means of 'free thinking' or 'brainstorming' sessions. (This is not the only method and much quiet thinking by everybody pays dividends.)

The results from these sessions are extremely gratifying—ideas are produced which did not exist in that particular form in any of the minds of the people present. There is an amplification of ideas. It is a difficult process to appreciate until one has experienced it and:

It is nothing to do with design by committee.

We say more on this subject later.

When the equipment upon which value analysis is to be performed has been chosen, a team of appropriate experts is gathered together. A good working number is six to eight; much smaller than six loses impetus while larger than eight gets ponderous. The value co-ordinator should be relieved of note taking as he must be continually alert to provide 'flywheel' action should the sessions falter in any way.

We will return to the individual members and the sessions after we have detailed the procedure disciplines. These are vital as they are instrumental in assisting the team to succeed.

They consist of six stages of work:

INFORMATION KEY TECHNIQUE 5 Know the costs. This is one of the first tasks for the value co-ordinator, to get *all* cost information on the product and product parts.

IDEAS STAGE This is where the team carries out speculative free thinking of ideas—Brainstorming.

IDEAS ASSEMBLY STAGE The ideas produced at the previous stage are investigated thoroughly and alternative solutions proposed.

RECOMMENDATION STAGE Recommendations are made by the value co-ordinator to the team and any last changes included and tidied up.

ACTION OR IMPLEMENTATION STAGE Formal change requests are issued into the company manufacturing change system.

CHECKING OR MONITOR STAGE The value co-ordinator must check that changes are going forward properly and that eventually the results are as expected.

We will now deal in more detail with the stages of work.

FIRST STAGE
The first task of the value co-ordinator and his assistants consists of a detailed analysis of the product and product part costs:

Cost of every part.
Cost of major parts.
Cost of functional groups of parts.
Quantity to be manufactured over how many years.
Relationship with similar products in the company range.
How costs are built up, how company overheads are applied, and what cost charges in labour and materials are likely.

This stage is exceedingly important, as without full details ideas for improving the value cannot be costed. Much assistance will be needed from the cost estimating section and manufacturing unit. In the process it will be unusual if it is not discovered that some weak areas of costing exist. There are sure to be lessons learnt because this

174

time we will not be assembling costs as estimating departments usually do, but dissecting them. The results can sometimes be interesting. At all times, however, the sections concerned must have confidence that comments on weaknesses will be made to them first.

SECOND STAGE

The first essential is that the value co-ordinator should learn something about the possible members of the team. He is likely to have to discuss the people with the managements concerned and has a difficult task ahead for the first meeting or two, as all are going to work in a way none of them has worked before. The members in a typical electronic engineering value analysis team would include:

Sales Engineer.
Purchasing Representative.
Production Engineer.
Quality Engineer.
Design Engineer.
Draughtsman.
Value analysis assistant (engineering or production background).
Value analysis co-ordinator.

The people should not be too junior and preferably with some ability to adjust to new situations. Above all, they must be very skilled in their respective professions.

When they meet for the first time it should be after all the individuals have had some lectures or training in the essential disciplines of value analysis. The value co-ordinator must reiterate the difference between these sessions and a normal meeting.

At these free thought sessions people must be encouraged to talk freely about their ideas, however 'way out' they seem; there must be no adverse criticism at this time from any other member. The value co-ordinator must see that an acceleration of ideas takes place. Out of this session will come new ideas and ways of achieving the function. Only after this, at the ideas assembly or investigation stage does the question of constructive criticism arise.

What sort of areas are likely to be covered in these sessions? Alternative methods of achieving the same function will come under the following general headings, although no single list could be claimed to be exhaustive:

> Elimination of parts, assemblies, processes or operations. This must always be the first aim, *elimination*.
>
> Simplification of parts, assemblies, processes or operations. This may be without affecting the intrinsic design of the sub-section of the whole design.
>
> Simplification of design in any part, assembly or piece to bring in new manufacturing methods.
>
> Examination of the company or bought out standard parts in place of special design.
>
> Simplification of manufacturing processes in relation to change of process, elimination of part of the process or type of plant used for the process, e.g. unnecessary polishing, cheaper casting methods or more automatic processing.
>
> Relaxation of tolerances and demands on accuracy in the manufacturing process to lower costs, use cheaper plant and lower rejections.
>
> Finding cheaper materials of equal merit to the original.
>
> Finding better materials which although more costly in themselves save money by their use in a different design.
>
> Examination of bought out parts rather than made in.
>
> Looking at all current technologies that might improve the value.

In our experience it is convenient to run several products at once and sessions were thus used for various purposes. This helps to break the sessions up as there is not much doubt that run properly there is a form of excitement generated in the flow of ideas formulation. The change of activity prevents a diminishing return from the session.

THIRD STAGE
This is where all the cost information is needed in order that the ideas accumulated at the second stage can be costed in detail and further discussed. Costing information is, of course, required in the second stage but only as an aid to the ideas and not to provide

comparisons, which might prevent a line of thought from being developed.

There will be further development at this stage of the ideas produced in the second stage; it should not be avoided and is likely to be beneficial. Eventually, however, there comes an assembly of the most appropriate ideas to date put back to the value co-ordinator for more precise costing and presentation to the members in a formal way.

FOURTH STAGE

Positive recommendations are made to the members showing the savings in cost or improvement in value generally. If they are approved the fifth and sixth stages can be carried out by the value co-ordinator.

Example of Cases

Some examples follow of value analysis in which we have been involved and which also conveniently show suitable documentation. Figures 12.1 and 12.2 are single activities. Figure 12.4 shows a graph of the calculated savings achieved from the first year's value analysis activities, while Fig. 12.3 is a summary sheet showing how the totals are made up. The graph in Fig. 12.4 would be modified by the second year's work and any changes in production quantities. The examples are:

A printer ribbon take up spool was made in the factory for £2 10s. 0d. A similar item cost 12s. from the supplier after a simplified design we helped to develop! There is worse to come: we sent spools back for 3s. credit! If you think this sort of thing can only happen to other people have a close look at everything you do in your company!

We bought a device from a manufacturer which always included a spare electrical plug. We never used the plug and eventually got £16 per device credit. Somebody used their eyes and saved the company a worthwhile total of money.

In a circuit design used for another purpose several components were more than capable of fulfilling the task. Smaller rating components were quite adequate and saved 6s. per circuit.

N

Description of part/assembly Output Unit 702912 Power supply. Type 3.	V.A. ref. no. 147 Sheet no: 1 of 2 Issue: 1 Date: 18.8.19...

V.A. proposal	Alternative method of mounting using slotted bars. Dispense the existing heat sink and mount transistors directly on component board made from aluminium. Replace turret lugs with insulated prestincerts, secure capacitor with Ty-rap in place of "P" clip.

Machine types affected:

Stock level: and WIP covered up to end of March 19....	Estimated implementation date: April, 19....

up to end

Machines programmed after implementation date: 192 up to end

Cost of existing parts: _ _ _) See _ _ _ _ _ _ _ _ _ _ _ _ _ _ _
Estimated cost of new part: _ ⎰Sheet 2⎱ _ _ _ _ _ _ _ No. per m/c _ _ 1 _ _ _ _
Estimated saving per m/c: _ _ £2.79 _ _ _ _ _ _ _ _ _

Gross estimated saving: _ _ _ _ _ _ _ _ _ _ _ _ _ _ _ _ £ 536

Cost of new drawings and
cost of change: _ _ _ _ _ _ _ _ _ _ _ _ £ 50 _ _ _ _ _ _ _ _.
New tooling: — _ _ _ _ _ _ _ _ _ _ _ £ 55 _ _ _ _ _ _ _.
Scrapped/modified tooling: — _ _ £ ⎫
Scrap parts: — _ _ _ _ _ _ _ _ _ _ £ ⎬ Nil
Other items: — _ _ _ _ _ _ _ _ _ _ £ ⎭

Total implementation costs: £ 105

Estimated actual saving: £ 431

Recommended action by V.A. team:

Change proposal to be raised

Confirmed actual saving: £ _ _ _ _ _ _ _ _

Date:

Fig. 12.1 Value analysis cost statement

Value analysis team proposal cost statement detail sheet			
	. V.A. ref. no.: 147		
	Sheet 2 of 2 issue 1		
Delete			
702912	Strip	— 2 off	0·638
770147	Lug	— 8 off	0·0368
702914	Board	— 4 off	2·2572
770120	P clip	— 4 off	0·0780
702915	Heat sink	— 4 off	0·7352
	Screws	— 26 off	0·026
	Nuts	— 26 off	0·026
	Washers	— 26 off	0·026
86204	Terminals	— 28 off	0·135
			3·9582
Add			
	Board aluminium	— 4 off	0·400
	Prestincerts	— 28 off	0·525
	Insulok tie	— 4 off	0·040
	Slotted bar	— 2 off	0·200
			1·165
			£
		Saving	2·7932

Fig. 12.2 Value analysis cost statement detail sheet

Value Engineering

This term is usually applied to value analysis type work applied to the product before manufacture, i.e. in the complete design and development stages.

There is no substitute for the utmost attack on the concept, specification and design and development of a product. While the product is in the very early stages the costs, methods of manufacture, performance and ultimate marketability are being fixed. This is the cheapest time to make changes; put the maximum design effort into the task and get it right.

179

Value analysis ref. no. and change no.	Description	Gross saving per machine	Machines affected by change, as fraction of output, e.g. $\frac{200}{500}$			Implementation cost	Potential net saving	All changes potential accumulated savings
			Yr. 1	Yr. 2	Yr. 3			
		£				£	£	£
	Brought forward from Sheet 5.							61,274
V.A. 136 CSB–P–079	Simplification of H.S. units punch power supply	25·25	Nil	$\frac{47}{79}$	$\frac{90}{90}$	145	3315	64,589
V.A. 137 CSB–P–079	Fascia panel, resistor mounting, etc. punch power supply	0·826	Nil	$\frac{47}{79}$	$\frac{90}{90}$	31·25	82	64,671
V.A. 140 CSB–P–079	Capacitor reduction punch power supply	2·83	Nil	$\frac{47}{79}$	$\frac{90}{90}$	10·0	378	65,049
V.A. 138 CSB–P–092	Hinge assembly punch power supply	1·66	Nil	$\frac{47}{79}$	$\frac{90}{90}$	20	208	65,257
V.A. 139 CSB–P–091	Capacitor board punch power supply	1·14	Nil	$\frac{47}{79}$	$\frac{90}{90}$	57	99	65,356
V.A. 141 CSB–P–097	Capacitor tray punch power supply	8·10	Nil	$\frac{47}{79}$	$\frac{90}{90}$	85	1025	66,381
V.A. 143 CSB–P–097	Fuse chassis punch power supply	1·45	Nil	$\frac{47}{79}$	$\frac{90}{90}$	17	181	66,562
V.A. 144 CSB–P–105	24V supply punch power supply	14·74	Nil	$\frac{47}{79}$	$\frac{90}{90}$	210	1810	68,372
							Carried forward	

Value analysis savings based on production programme N37

Compiled by – – – – – – – – – –   Date

Sheet 6 of 6 sheets

Fig. 12.3 Value analysis savings

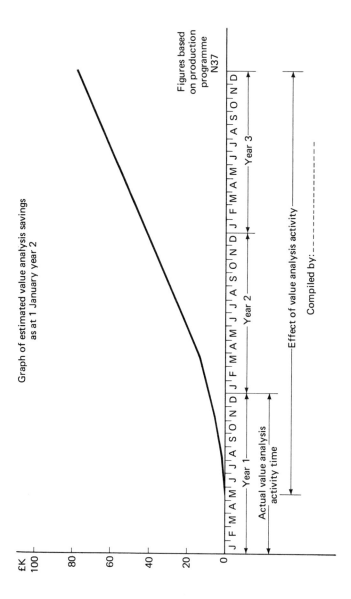

Fig. 12.4 Graph of estimated savings from complete N37 programme

Value engineering requires a separate small group of people to investigate the design and help the designers in much the same way as we have explained the second stage of value analysis. With value engineering the scope can be larger, as this is the time for the design and manufacturing processes to be turned inside out to find the best answers. There are, of course, always difficulties in timescales as the time grinds inexorably on and a late product may be an unrequired product or at best a poor seller. There is, therefore, the greatest reason for maximum effort right from the beginning. All too often the effort is applied when it is really too late.

The co-operation between the value engineering group and the design engineers must be very close and it is only to be expected that the latter are entitled to see worthwhile results from the extra effort. What are the sort of areas the value engineers attack?

The basic design function. Nothing must be sacred in trying to tear apart the design to see if there is a simpler, cheaper, better way of doing the job. Brainstorming sessions, design reviews and committees all have their place. The secret is drive, drive, drive to get the concept stage fully acceptable before moving on.

The same applies to detailed specifications. Attack the functions all the time.

In the design and development stage apply all the technology knowledge at your disposal. Ready access is essential, to information inside and outside the company. The right technology is one sure step to profits.

In detail, the areas of attack range from overall function to, say, a plating process for a small part. From the Purchasing Manager's well known graph of product cost, i.e. about 20 per cent of the parts by quantity equals about 75 per cent of the cost, Fig. 12.5, then the value engineer must look at the high cost group of items to get the maximum return over the least area.

BOUGHT OUT PARTS OR ITEMS
The value engineer should always make sure that by the correct specifications the company is getting the maximum benefit from

bought out items. Why were the parts bought out in the first instance? Whether the answer is because the resources would be strained to do it or because of inability to carry out the technology required, the result is the same: extra resources of men and machinery are being bought as required. If, however, the items are not specified correctly, there can either be an incredible waste of resources and/or the product function or cost is not as planned. Encourage the sub-contractor to join with you in achieving maximum value. Encourage him to suggest ways and means of solving the problem and stimulate his interest in your problem by fair profits for him with value control.

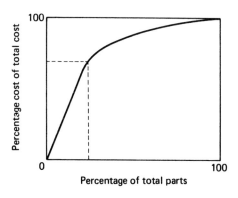

Fig. 12.5 Product cost curve, quantities vs. cost

Value Control

This book cannot cover the full scope of value engineering, but we hope the idea of value control is easy to appreciate. It is a state of never being satisfied unless costs are going down for a given function and quality or function and/or quality are being improved for the same cost. Figure 12.6 shows the familiar 'break even' chart with effects of quality and/or function adjustment.

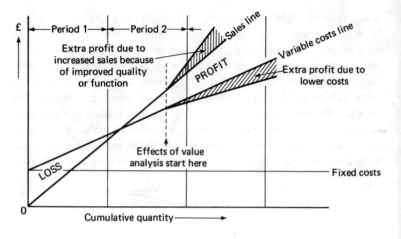

Fig. 12.6 Break even chart showing value analysis effects

thirteen The Contract

Is a Contract Necessary?
A great many projects are carried out on behalf of a customer by a main contractor. In such cases a key document for the Project Manager is the contract.

The first major point to consider is how far the contractor should be prepared to go without a contract. Some work will clearly be done before this to prepare a tender and possibly even some engineering development or laboratory work to determine the feasibility of aspects of the plan. This, however, must be done if there is to be any hope of securing the order. Once the decision to place an order is taken, how much work should be done before signing a contract?

If the project timescale is tight, and somehow it nearly always is, there is pressure to go ahead and start work without waiting for the paperwork. In some cases this may be justified though it always contains an element of danger. In the 1950's and early 1960's many computer projects were carried out without a contract ever being committed to paper and signed. Some firms have such close links with each other that they may feel they can go ahead without the formality of a contract. However, if delay over the contract is due to disagreement over the terms or details of the contract the disagreement will remain and may even be strengthened as the work proceeds. In our opinion it is always best to have a signed contract before anything more than planning is done. If you have to go ahead without a contract try to obtain written heads of agreement on the basis of the contract. This should contain agreement on the job to be done, the relevant dates and agreement on who pays for work done in anticipation of a contract.

Contract Commitments

Although the formalties of drawing up the contract are unlikely to be the concern of the Project Manager, he is vitally concerned with some of its contents. First he should review all dates quoted in the contract. Is it still possible to meet them or has there been so much delay in evaluating tenders that all dates must be revised? Ideally all dates quoted in tenders should be related to the date of Instruction to Proceed, e.g. completion on ITP date, plus 25 months. Unfortunately firm dates are frequently quoted and it is these which must be reviewed. This may lead to recriminations from the customer or your own firm's salesman, but it is madness to enter into a contract knowing that its performance is impossible of achievement. It is better to get the pain over at this stage. If the project is then completed in the time contracted for, you will be given full credit for it.

The Customer's Part

The next point to consider is whether your project performance is in any way dependent upon the customer. Customer dependencies should be extracted from your project PERT plan and listed with their dates. In a computer project, the customer may be required to have his building ready for the computer by a certain date. It must be quite clear what state of readiness is required. Is the customer for instance required to have the room prepared to a given environmental specification and is he required to have the air conditioning installed and satisfactorily passed through its acceptance tests?

If the customer is required to provide a detailed specification of work to be done, it must be quite clear in the contractual documents what is to be supplied and when. It must also be clearly agreed what is to happen in the event:

1 That the detailed specification differs materially from the invitation to tender.
2 That on detailed scrutiny of the specification, the contractor finds serious flaws in it.

186

Where a contract is undertaken on a cost plus basis it is desirable to cover these points. Where the contract is either fixed price or where part of the contract is on a fixed price basis, it is absolutely essential to be crystal clear on these points.

Where the customer is a government department it is necessary to watch what is presented as the specification. If they are running late, they may try to pass off draft specifications in an unchecked manuscript state. When the final typed or printed specification is received several weeks or even months later it may be found to differ significantly from the draft specifications. This can cause disruption to schedules. It may require some work to be redone. It may reflect a more complicated task than originally specified. If the specifications are voluminous, as they may well be for instance for the construction of an oil refinery, the mere task of reading the final specification and comparing it with the draft may well be an appreciable task in itself.

If the contract for your project is tied to a fixed delivery date or a fixed price it is absolutely essential to resist all pleas from the customer that the changes will only be little ones and that the contractor should be reasonable. Insist that any specifications are delivered on time and in the required form. If they are not, a formal letter recording the deviation from contract must be sent immediately and an acknowledgement asked for.

In some types of project it is, of course, unreasonable to expect that there will be no changes to specification during the life of the project. These, however, must be kept to a minimum as changes can be very disruptive to progress. Essential changes must be strictly controlled and recorded. The record must contain details of the changes, their effects and the date on which the customer and contractor agreed to the change. The implications on the cost and timescale of the project must be evaluated and agreed. Wherever possible this should be done before it is agreed to go ahead. The effect of changes should be agreed by the customer in writing and should bear the signature of a member of the customer's staff who is able to authorize expenditure.

Project Risks

Another area, which requires careful examination at the contract stage, is that of risk and insurance. The main contractor must be clear about and should define in the contract the extent of the risk he will bear. Where equipment is concerned the precise point at which risk passes must be established. In many cases this will be 'on acceptance' by the customer. Who carries the risk when there are accidents on site? Suppose an accident occurs, when a crane is lifting a piece of heavy equipment on site. The equipment is damaged so badly it has to go back to the factory for rebuilding, delaying the project completion by several months. One of your staff and one of the customer's staff are killed or injured in the accident. Considerable damage is also done to one of the customer's buildings. Delay to the project opens up the question of consequential loss. The effect of delay on the customer's business could be such as to cost him in the case of a large project hundreds of thousands of pounds a month and in total could be sufficient to put even a large and well established contractor out of business, if he accepts the risk and fails to insure against it. The Project Manager should try to identify all these risk areas. Agreement must then be reached between customer and contractor as to who carries the various risks at each stage in the project's life. Once this is agreed, it should be a straightforward matter to arrange the necessary insurance.

Money

An important aspect of the contract is the part dealing with payment. Payment, or part of the payment, may be related to acceptance tests. In this case there should be a contractual reference to the criteria and method of acceptance testing. The phasing of payment should, of course, have been considered at the time the price for the project was settled. Progress payments enable the contractor to finance his work in progress. In the end the decision on whether to have progress payments or not and how they should be phased is probably decided on the basis of which party has easiest access to funds and which party can raise money at the lowest rate of interest. These are two aspects of the same problem. For instance, if a computer company were to execute a large project for an established insurance company, it is probable that the insurance company would make progress payments in stages so as to cover the full cost of work in progress, thus avoiding the need for the computer company to raise additional loans to finance the project. The insurance company can clearly raise money more cheaply, at least in the United Kingdom, than the computer company. There is no point in forcing the computer company to finance the project if the result, in effect, is that the insurance company pays a concealed interest charge, higher than they would normally pay.

For some customers the question of payment is bound up with the question of trust. They feel that as long as they have not paid, they have a hold over their main contractor and can force him to accede to their wishes. Such an attitude is short sighted and does not hold out hope for a successful project. Apart from anything else, the contractor's staff are human and will try to recoup their losses elsewhere on the contract or on later extensions to it. However, the customer may well have a legitimate fear about the future maintenance of the project works. In any project involving complicated machinery or complex systems this will arise. The customer must sensibly protect himself by clauses ensuring continuity of supply of parts or of maintenance where the contractor takes responsibility for it. He should also ensure some agreement on price, preferably linking increases in price to some readily identifiable index. The contractor for his part is concerned to limit his future liability to maintain obsolescent machinery. In an industry such as computers even the computer manufacturer may have severe difficulty in obtaining stocks of obsolete components.

Linked with the question of maintenance is that of documentation. The customer naturally wants full and clear documentation. The extent of this should be agreed early on and adequate reference to it included in the contract. In the case of overseas contracts it may also be wise to define the language in which the documentation is to be written. For an English speaking firm there is a considerable difference in cost between delivering operating instructions in English and the same instructions in Arabic script. It may be necessary to do so—indeed the ability to do so may have helped to secure the contract in the first place. None the less it carries a cost, which must be reflected in the price. Hence if there is any possibility of doubt about the language in which the documentation will be written, the point should be covered in the contract. A linked point is the question of how many copies are required. In a very large project involving several shifts of operating and maintenance staff, there may be a heavy training commitment. Such a project may involve staff at a number of remote locations, as would be the case, for instance, where a network of remote terminals is involved. In such cases the question of the numbers of operating and other manuals to be provided should be covered in the contract. A software house undertook the programming for a project for a large organization in the United Kingdom. The value of the contract to them was rather less than £400,000. They planned to hand over the documentation of the system in the form of two typed copies of the program specification. At the end of the project this was in dispute and finally the software house had to hand over a considerable number of printed volumes of program specification. The cost to them of this additional work was about £8000 or 5 per cent of the total price. Needless to say this had an unfortunate effect on the profitability of the contract and one that might have been avoided, had the point been covered in the original contract.

Penalties

Penalties is a subject which is much discussed in connection with contracts. Strictly speaking penalties cannot be enforced in English law. What are generally referred to as penalty clauses do not in effect provide for the payment of penalties. They provide for the payment of liquidated damages. The parties concerned consider what damage the customer will suffer in the event of late delivery and put a price on it. This means that should there be a delay in completion, all that need be established is the fact of delay. The liquidated damages—or the penalty in common usage—becomes payable, provided the contractor does not allege the fault of the customer as the reason for the delay. In fact the presence of a 'penalty clause' can act as a protection for a contractor. In the early hopeful stages of a contract, the customer can usually be tied down to a level of penalties well below the actual damage he will suffer in the event of serious delay.

Most contractors try to avoid a penalty clause in the hope that the customer will not go to law for damages in the event of delay. If he does, they hope the responsibility for delay will be sufficiently unclear to protect them.

However, where a contractor accepts a penalty clause there are some points he should watch. He should try to secure a period following the target delivery date, during which he will not be liable for penalties. He should try to exclude penalties for delay as a result of circumstances beyond his control. Delays which may result from the customer's failure to perform should be identified and excluded. The total size of penalty must always be restricted. It is foolish to enter into any contract with a penalty clause which can cream off more than your profit on that contract. Every penalty should have a maximum figure put on it in the contract. Something between 5 and 10 per cent of the contract price is quite common. Even within this total action should be taken to spread the penalty, e.g. by making it come into effect on the basis of say $\frac{1}{4}$ per cent for each week of delay. This has advantages to both parties. For the contractor the advantage is obvious. The customer also gains from the spur to the contractor to keep the delay to a minimum. If the penalty were payable as a lump sum after 4 weeks delay, the contractor would have less incentive to complete the project once he had gone 4 weeks late and incurred the full penalty.

Some large organizations make it a rule always to include a penalty clause in all their project contracts. This can rebound on them if they become too well known for both insisting on the penalty clause and for unreasonable interpretation of it. In such circumstances, contractors merely add the full cost of the penalty into their costs when establishing the price to tender.

Where a customer insists on a penalty clause, the contractor should equally firmly insist on placing on the customer any extra costs he may incur as a result of the customer's default in performance. These extra—or overrun costs as they are sometimes known—can be considerable. The cost of project staff salaries and interest costs on capital employed can on their own be a substantial amount for even a week of delay on a large project.

Linked to the question of penalties is that of cancellation. Normally the contractor having signed a contract has no right to withdraw from the contract. The customer sometimes insists on the right to cancel in certain circumstances. For instance a contract for the execution of a project over a period of 2 years might include a penalty provision of £10,000 a week up to a maximum of £520,000. This might be linked to a provision for cancellation of the contract and repayment of all progress payments which had been made. Probably the right to cancel would be given after 52 weeks delay, i.e. after full payment of penalties. This is quite a reasonable provision. If the contractor planned to do the work in 2 years and failed to do it in three, he may well be incompetent to complete it. The delay to completion may be due to inability to get the project up to acceptance test standards. Without provision for cancellation the project might drag on indefinitely without satisfaction to either party. If the project is within sight of satisfactory completion it is unlikely that the customer will exercise his right to cancel—unless, of course, he has had second thoughts about the value of the project!

Prepare for the Worst

There are those who say one should always hope for the best and be prepared for the worst. In the project world, the contract is where all parties are prepared for the worst. If the project goes well, the copies of the contract will be put in their respective files and gather dust. If the contract goes wrong, it will be pulled out and gone over word by word. A court of law or an arbitrator may be involved and an interpretation put on every comma.

fourteen The Consortium Project

Why get involved in a Consortium?

One of the most exciting and challenging opportunities for Project Managers lies in the field of consortium operations. In a normal project if anything can go wrong, it will. In a consortium project the chance of things going wrong is many times as great.

A consortium project is one in which two or more companies undertake a project jointly. There are many reasons for doing this rather than for one company going it alone. The scope of a project may be too wide for one company to handle on its own. It may not have adequate resources, knowhow or finance to tender for the project. A company may feel that tendering on its own, it is just not credible to the customer. Companies which compete in the home market may decide to pool their efforts for large overseas projects, on the basis that a share of the cake is better than none at all.

There are particular circumstances in overseas markets which favour consortium operations. The central buying organizations of Iron Curtain countries like their projects to be with a single contractor, who has full responsibility for the successful completion of the contract. In some cases this result can be achieved by placing a contract with one company, who in turn places subcontracts for some of the work. In many cases, however, this relationship puts too great a risk on the shoulders of the main contractor. In others such a relationship is inappropriate between the companies con-

o

cerned. Underdeveloped countries also often require tenders from a single contractor—one company or a consortium of companies. In this case they are frequently seeking sound management as a guarantee of the success of their project. In fact they want to buy project management.

Consortium Problems

Project management either on behalf of a consortium or for one of the member companies is different. All the basic techniques used in normal project management are used, but additional elements are met. These are conflicts of interest and misunderstanding. For the Project Manager himself and for his staff, there may also be a conflict of loyalties.

Conflict of Interest

When companies join together in a consortium to undertake a project, they have a common interest in the success of that project. However, the extent of that interest and its importance to the individual companies may vary. To one company, the project may be vital and the profit from the project may be of substantial importance to it. To another member of the consortium it may just be one more marginal item in its operations. Profit margins to the companies concerned may well differ.

When the individual parent companies consider taking on other projects they are likely to give main consideration to their own interests, even if this has an adverse effect on the consortium project. These possible conflicts of interest must be fully appreciated at the time the consortium is set up. Before the tender to the potential customer is made, an agreement should be reached on the main responsibilities of the partners in the consortium and this should be committed to writing. It will be one of the key guides for the Project Manager. If he has been appointed at this stage, he should study the document with care and try to ensure that it covers the essentials. Among the more obvious items are provision for managing the project, terms on which profits are to be shared, the contribution of staff, provision of finance and resources. There are, however, some less obvious but extremely important items which must be covered.

These include the means by which the consortium may be dissolved or by which one or more members may withdraw before the completion of the project. One hopes that all the members of the consortium have entered it in good faith. There is, however, always the possibility that under the stress of difficulty and possible losses and penalties, one member may try to avoid his liabilities by withdrawing. As in so many other fields, one should go forward hoping for the best, but covering the worst in the contingency plans.

PENALTIES

Another item which should be covered in the consortium agreement is the question of penalties. A member of the consortium who makes a comparatively minor contribution by value—say 5 per cent of the contract—can by late delivery or by failure to meet the specification bring about penalties on the full amount of the contract. It is no consolation to the other members that he is paying his 5 per cent share of the penalties if they are paying penalties, when their own contribution has been made up to specification and on time.

SEPARATE TENDERS

Will individual members of the consortium submit separate tenders or subcontract to other firms, submitting tenders for the same project? At first sight the answer appears to be 'no'. The very suggestion seems disloyal to the conception of a consortium. You may say, can one firm have its heart in more than one tender for the same job? Nonetheless there may be special cases where a consortium member may legitimately wish to take part in more than one consortium tendering for the same project. If this should be so, the matter should be covered in the written agreement setting up the consortium. At the least, any firm submitting a separate tender should be required to notify the consortium if it does so. It should also agree that it will give the consortium at least as good—and preferably better—terms than it gives in any separate tender. These terms should include delivery, maintenance and training arrangements as well as price.

If the Project Manager starts his project with a soundly constructed consortium agreement it will make his very difficult job at least possible. Throughout the project, however, he must bear in mind the possible conflicts of interest of the parties involved. Their effects may well be made worse by suspicion and misunderstanding.

Can your Consortium Colleagues be Trusted?

There is usually some background of suspicion. Has one company got a better deal from the consortium than another? Are the conditions of the contract more onerous on one member? Is one company obtaining more than its fair share of influence in arriving at consortium decisions by barely concealed blackmail? All these thoughts, and many far more petty, will occur. The Project Manager must be on his guard against them all the time and must take positive action to disarm any possible suspicion.

You may think that if people say or write quite straightforwardly what they think, and what they are prepared to do, there can be no misunderstanding. Even if all consortium members have a common language they can misunderstand each other. Every industry and profession has its own jargon. Unfortunately the same word can mean different things to different people. To people in the computer industry a multiplexor means one thing, while it means something entirely different to people in the electronic communications field. Even people in the same industry may attach different meanings to words such as 'compatible' and 'modular'.

Words may have more than one meaning. To a woman 'make up' is a matter of cosmetics, but to someone in the printing industry 'make up' is an expression with a well defined technical meaning, relating to the preparation of a page of print. If you think about it the words 'make up' can be used to mean a number of different things, depending upon the context in which they are used, e.g. fabricate a story or make peace after a quarrel. Even in the 1970's differences in regional background and education can result in misunderstanding over the use of words.

When the consortium contains firms of several different nationalities the possibilities of misunderstanding are compounded. Good interpreters are rare and many mistakes are made. It is worse still if a representative of one firm prides himself on his knowledge of a foreign language, an Englishman for instance who likes to show off his knowledge of French or German. He may unwittingly enter into commitments which he neither intended to nor is capable of carrying out.

196

One way in which the Project Manager will make his own life much easier is to try to prevent misunderstandings arising. Where he does not succeed, the misunderstanding must be unravelled as soon as possible. Remember, no one likes to be told that he doesn't know what he is talking about, or that he can't understand the Queen's English. It will take longer to persuade people to explain what they mean clearly and simply, but if this is done tactfully it will leave no hard feelings and will contribute to the successful and profitable completion of the project.

Can a Man serve two Masters?

A consortium may be set up in many different ways. It is quite common for it to take the legal form of a partnership, or of a limited liability company. In such cases a board or management committee will be established consisting of senior managers, representing each company in the consortium. This will probably meet fairly infrequently, possibly once a month. The day to day work will be delegated to the consortium Project Manager (or Managing Director or General Manager—titles may vary). In the majority of cases he will be an executive of one of the companies in the consortium, lent to the consortium to manage the consortium project. There will be different considerations where a consortium is being set up with the intention of handling a number of projects or a particular class of business. Here we are concerned with the single project consortium, lasting perhaps 2 to 5 years. In almost all such cases, the Project Manager comes from one of the constituent companies of the consortium. He may have almost no staff of his own and work through the project Managers of the individual companies. If he does require a staff, this may be provided by the individual companies or if time permits some staff may be specifically recruited on short contract, and be employed by the consortium itself.

The Project Manager and, to a lesser extent, the other seconded staff have to face the problem of divided loyalties. This is not unique to consortium Project Managers but is also a problem to the staff of multi-national organizations. The Project Manager is now employed and paid for by the consortium. His objective is the successful completion of the project on behalf of the consortium. However, he cannot escape his ties to his own company, which probably still deals with his own personal administration. His salary may be a charge to the consortium, but is probably physically paid by his own company. He belongs to its pension fund and still has all the benefits which it may offer to members of its management staff. In due course he will expect to go back into his own company, and to be given an appropriate post in its management structure—hopefully involving promotion as a result of the successful completion of the consortium project. However, his own company's interest, at some stage in the project, may be at variance with that of the consortium due to an earlier miscalculation or due to circumstances arising in another part of the company's business. The management of his own company may bring pressure to bear on him to accept what is really not in the consortium's best interest. To the Project Manager this can be a very dangerous situation, particularly for a man in his forties or fifties. However, there is really only one course for him to pursue. His responsibility is to the consortium and he himself will be judged by the success or failure of the project. He must take the course which he believes is the right one for the consortium. His own company's management will not respect him if he succumbs to their blackmail. In any case the man who brings a large consortium project to success-ful fruition is a rare man, who can command a high price in the market.

An Opportunity for Profit

We have stressed the problems of a consortium project and they are real and very costly when they are overlooked. The fact remains, however, that the prime reason for forming any consortium is that it offers an opportunity for profit to each of its members, which individually would not otherwise be open to them. Within the United Kingdom all the nuclear power station construction is undertaken by one or other of the powerful consortia formed to handle this type of work. No individual company can compete against the consortia in this field. Some of the largest and most powerful companies in the world find it worth their while to form consortia to handle large complicated projects. Bethlehem Steel and Rio Tinto Zinc Corporation have joined forces to handle the Churchill Falls power project in Canada, one of the largest power projects ever undertaken and which will cost over a thousand million dollars when it is completed.

Companies such as these form consortia to undertake projects they could not otherwise touch. They do it because it pays.

part four Project Choice

fifteen The Financial Evaluation

ONE OF THE MAIN preoccupations of management is the allocation of scarce resources. These resources include skilled management and staff, capital equipment and cash. For every project management must ask itself, 'Are the resources available?' It should also ask, 'Is this the best use to which these resources can be put?'

Most projects are subjected to an evaluation before they are given the go-ahead. An essential part of this evaluation is the financial appraisal. Traditionally this has been aimed at deciding whether or not a project will be profitable and selecting which of several competing projects appears the most profitable. However, as we shall see in the course of this section modern techniques go further than this. They go right inside a project and help management to decide on the precise shape of the project as well as highlighting those aspects of a project which will warrant particular attention for management.

In large organizations the financial appraisal of projects is probably made by central planning or accounting staff. Even in these cases the Project Manager should understand the processes so that he can benefit from them.

Traditional Methods

The traditional ways of evaluating projects have been the return on investment method and the payback period method. Although as we shall see there are much more effective methods available these two traditional methods are still widely used. This is just as true of the sleepy giants of industry as it is of the smaller companies and organizations.

The advantage of the traditional methods is their simplicity. Unfortunately, as we shall see, they often provide a false basis for decision.

Because of this many investment decisions are made which are fundamentally wrong. Projects which can never be profitable are undertaken. Expenditure is incorrectly placed. Manpower is sometimes used where capital, i.e. machinery, should have been used.

Before going on to more sophisticated methods let us look first at the traditional methods.

RATE OF RETURN (RR)

Probably the most popular of the traditional methods of financial evaluation is the rate of return method. Here the expected profit is expressed as a percentage rate of return on the initial capital investment. Expected profit is usually estimated often allowing for depreciation but before tax. A variation on this method is to take the average capital employed rather than the initial capital.

To take a simple example, £1000 is invested in a project with a 5 year life. The project earns £160 a year before tax but after depreciation in each of the 5 years, i.e. £800 in all. We assume that the residual value of the investment is nil at the end of the 5 years. The rate of return is:

$$\frac{\text{Earnings}}{\text{Capital} \times \text{Number of years}} \times 100 \text{ per cent}$$
$$= \frac{800 \times 100}{1000 \times 5} \text{ per cent} = 16 \text{ p.a. rate of return}$$

The rate of return method suffers from the following disadvantages:

1 It takes no account of the timing of payments and receipts.
2 Because the RR method takes no account of tax and is based on initial capital employed, it does not give a true rate of return on capital employed and is, therefore, not a true yardstick by which to judge which projects will be profitable.

THE PAYBACK METHOD (PB)

This is the simplest method of investment appraisal. It is the number of years which are taken to pay back the initial investment from the trading surplus. Normally the calculation is made ignoring both depreciation and tax. The payback method suffers from the following disadvantages:

1 It takes no account of earnings which are expected to be received after the payback period.
2 It takes no account of the timing of receipts and payments within the payback period.
3 Like the RR method, ignoring tax gives a false picture. A project with an excellent payback period of 3 years in gross terms may have a comparatively short life thereafter and in after tax terms may never be profitable.

Years	0	1	2	3	4	5	6
				£			
Project A	−100	20	20	20	20	20	20
Project B	−100	35	35	20	5	5	20

Two projects A and B both have an initial capital cost of £100 and both earn £120 over 6 years. The payback method indicates that both projects have a payback period of 5 years. They will also have identical rates of return (RR), i.e. £20 on an initial investment of £100, that is 20 per cent RR.

The Need for More Effective Methods

Both PB and RR rate project A and B identically although it should be clear that project B has a considerable advantage in the timing of its earnings. After 3 years it is expected to have earned £90 against the £60 earned by project A.

This simple example shows that although the traditional methods of appraisal give some indication of profitability they do not give any weight to returns which are earned in the near as opposed to the more remote future. They clearly fail to distinguish between the two projects.

To distinguish between projects we need a method which will reflect the time value of money and for this purpose the discounting methods have been developed.

sixteen Discounting Methods

Discounting Methods are not New

Discounting methods of investment appraisal have been in use by the discriminating few for nearly a century. It was in 1877 that Hoskold's book, *Engineer's Valuing Assistant*, a practical treatise on the valuation of collieries and other mines, was first published. In this book he described a discounting method of investment appraisal. However, to the majority of managements discounting methods were unknown until they were rediscovered in the late 1950's. Even now they are not as widely used as they might be.

The discounting techniques of investment appraisal overcome the disadvantages of the traditional methods. They produce a single figure, which gives a value ranking to an investment project.

Discounting techniques are founded on two simple concepts:

1 Money has a time value. Money in the hand today is worth more than the same money in the hand in a year's time. This reflects the fact that capital has a price, i.e. interest and also that the value of money is eroded by inflation.
2 Investment in a project is concerned with cash rather than entries in the conventional account books.

The Time Value of Money

What will the value of £100 in the hand be in a year's time? In simple terms it will be £100 plus 1 year's interest. If the rate of interest is 10 per cent, it will be £110. What will be the present value of £100 received in a year's time? In simple terms it will be £100 minus 1 year's interest. If the rate of interest is 10 per cent, it will be £90·91. The reason that it is £90·91 rather than £90 is simple. £90 plus 10 per cent interest is only £99. To obtain the exact figure we say,

$$£100 = £x + 10 \text{ per cent of } £x = 1·1x$$

So x, the discounted figure for which we are looking $= \dfrac{£100}{1·1}$

However, most people once they know how to do the calculation will prefer to use tables to find the answer. A discount table is given in the Appendix. If you look down the left hand column to a rate of 10 per cent and trace across the table to the 1 year column you find a figure of 0·9091. This is the value of £1 discounted over 1 year at a rate of 10 per cent per year. Therefore, for £100 we find £90·91. These tables are calculated on a compound interest basis for a number of years over a range of interest rates.

Net Present Value (NPV)

NPV is used to compare project investments in a quantitative manner. A rate of interest is selected on which the calculations are based. This rate should normally be the rate which represents the cost of money to an organization or a rate which represents the minimum rate of return on capital acceptable to the organization. The cash flows expected over the life of a project are set down. They are then discounted at the selected rate of interest and the net present value of each cash flow item is obtained. The sum of these net present values gives the project NPV.

NPV Simple Example

Project C involves the outlay of £500 at the beginning of the period. Thereafter at the end of each year the project earns £100, £200, £200, £200, £100. It ceases to earn after 5 years and there is no residual value. Using an interest rate of 10 per cent in the table in the Appendix, we calculate as follows:

Year	£ Cash Flow	£ NPV
0	−500	−500
1	100	+ 91
2	200	+165
3	200	+150
4	200	+137
5	100	+ 62
	+300	+105

Note that capital and income have been treated simply as negative and positive cash flows. For the sake of simplicity, all figures have been taken to the nearest whole £1.

The result of our calculation is that project C after allowing for repayment of the capital invested in it will yield a net present value of £105. It is this figure which is then used for comparison with the NPV calculated for other projects.

How, for instance, does project C compare with project D where the earnings are greater, but slower to come in. The annual earnings are £nil, £100, £150, £300, £300. Going to the tables and using the same 10 per cent rate we get:

Year	£ Cash Flow	£ NPV
0	−500	−500
1	Nil	—
2	100	+ 83
3	150	+113
4	300	+205
5	300	+186
	+350	+87

The NPV of project D is only £87 compared with £105 for project C and hence project C is to be preferred on financial grounds.

Using traditional methods we would have reached the same conclusion with the payback method but the opposite conclusion using rate of return. Another way of looking at NPV is to consider the project as a bank account with a nil balance. The first capital outflow creates an overdraft which is reduced by receipts from the projects earnings and increased by interest payments on the overdraft. At the end of the project the account is either in credit or still overdrawn by a certain amount. The NPV is that amount, adjusted to take account of the time value of money.

NPV Profiles

A useful way of presenting the net present values for a project in chart form is an NPV profile. Figure 16.1 illustrates an NPV profile for project E. The calculations for the profile are:

Year		Cash value Actual	NPV at discount rate of:			
			5%	10%	15%	20%
0	—	£20,000	−20,000	−20,000	−20,000	−20,000
1	+	4000	+ 3810	3636	3478	3333
2	+	6000	+ 5442	4958	4537	4166
3	+	6000	+ 5183	4508	3945	3472
4	+	5000	+ 4114	3415	2859	2412
5	+	4000	+ 3134	2484	1989	1608
6	+	2000	+ 1492	1129	865	670
NPV	£	7000	+ £3175	+£ 130	−£2327	−£4339

As the discount rate increases, so the NPV falls. When NPV = 0, the discount rate is the DCF rate for the project.

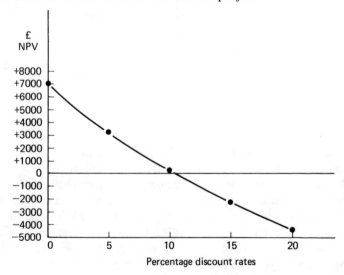

Fig. 16.1 NPV profile

Profiles for alternative projects can be plotted on the same graph.

Alternatively, profiles can be drawn to the same scale on transparent paper and overlaid. This may be particularly valuable when a number of projects are being considered or when a number of alternative methods of undertaking a project are being evaluated.

NPV Time Profiles

In some projects a major uncertainty is the earning life of the project. In these cases it may be helpful to draw an NPV time profile showing the NPV at a given discount rate. The assumption is made that the only alteration to the NPV if the project is reduced is that the cash flow for the 'lost' period is also lost.

Project E is drawn as an NPV time profile in Fig. 16.2 with a discount rate of 10 per cent.

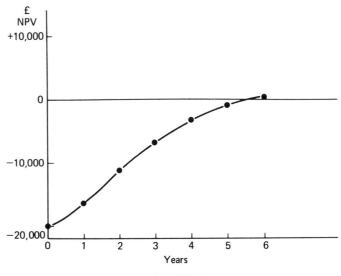

Fig. 16.2 NPV time

The figures are derived from the previous project E table. The NPV figures in the 10 per cent column are used. A cumulative NPV at the end of each year is given in the table below. For year 1 this is calculated by taking —£20,000 +£3636 which gives —£16,364 and so on for the following years.

	£ —
Life of project in years	NPV
0	— £20,000
1	— 16,364
2	— 11,406
3	— 6898
4	— 3483
5	— 999
6	+ 130

Such a profile helps to underline the risks involved should the life of the project be curtailed. If there is a possibility that income might continue after the sixth year, this should also be illustrated on the profile.

NPV for Comparing Costs

The NPV technique can be used to evaluate:

1 Projects which do not directly earn an income, e.g. provision of new office equipment.
2 Alternative methods of implementing the same project, e.g. to rent or buy equipment or plant.

As an example we consider a simplified case of whether to buy or rent a computer on the following assumptions:

Purchase: Price less investment grant £178,800.

Life 5 years with residual value £3000.

Annual maintenance and insurance cost £5000.

Rental: Annual rental including maintenance and insurance £60,000.

Residual value after 5 years nil.

It can be seen from Fig. 16.3 that in this particular case it would pay to rent rather than purchase if the cost of capital to the company is greater than 17·5 per cent.

PURCHASE

DISCOUNT FACTORS

Year	Cash flow £000	5% NPV £000	10% NPV £000	15% NPV £000	20% NPV £000
0	178	178	178	178	178
1	5	4·8	4·5	4·3	4·2
2	5	4·5	4·1	3·8	3·5
3	5	4·3	3·8	3·3	2·9
4	5	4·1	3·4	2·8	2·4
5	2	1·6	1·2	1·0	0·8
	200	197·3	195·0	193·2	191·8

RENTAL

1	60	57·1	54·5	52·2	50·0
2	60	54·4	49·6	45·4	41·7
3	60	51·8	45·1	39·5	34·7
4	60	49·4	41·0	34·3	28·9
5	60	47·0	37·3	29·8	24·1
	300	259·7	227·5	201·2	179·4

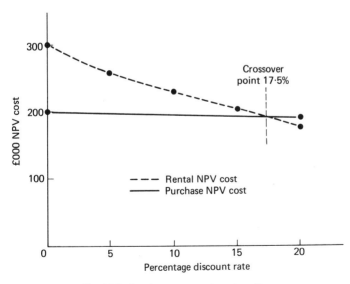

Fig. 16.3 Purchase vs. rental cost profile

211

In a comparison of this sort profiles would probably also be compiled for a number of different life spans.

Discounted Cash Flow (DCF)

When calculating the NPV of a project we have assumed a rate of return and used this as an entry point into the discount tables. Another approach is to consider what rate of return will be obtained over the life of a project such that the NPV = 0. This rate of return is known as the internal rate of return or the Discounted Cash Flow (DCF) rate of return.

In practice DCF is frequently preferred to NPV because it gives one figure for each project, which can be compared not only against the DCF for other projects but also against the company's yardstick rate. It also provides an indication of the maximum rate you can afford to pay for the capital to finance a particular project.

Essentially, the DCF technique involves calculating the time adjusted, net of tax, rate of return on the capital invested in a project. Under DCF the annual net earnings are regarded as part repayment of capital and part interest on the outstanding capital balance. This concept should be quite familiar to anyone who has a repayment mortgage from a Building Society. Under such a mortgage the rate of interest is calculated at such a rate that the balance outstanding on the mortgage becomes nil after a fixed number of years and the payments cease.

The DCF rate of return is the rate of return, in each year of the project's life, on the amount of capital which remains invested in that project. In project F the initial capital expenditure is £1000 and £620 is the amount of earnings at the end of year 1. A final payment of £560 is received at the end of years 2. This can be set out as follows:

	Col. 1	Col. 2	Col. 3	Col. 4	Col. 5
Years	Capital Balance at Start of Year (£)	Earnings in Year	Notional Interest for Year @ 12%	Balance of Earnings used to repay Capital	Capital Balance at End of Year
1	1000	+620	−120	+500	500
2	500	+560	− 60	+500	0

212

Although the calculation of a DCF rate is laborious it is quite simple. All that is involved is to enter the discount tables on a trial and error basis until the DCF rate is obtained, i.e. the rate at which the NPV = 0. (In the above example, 12 per cent.)

In project C we used a 10 per cent rate and obtained an NPV of £105. To find the DCF rate we will use the same cash flow figures, but with varying discounts until NPV = 0.

Year	Cash Flow	NPV at Discount Rate of:			
		10%	15%	17%	18%
0	− £500	− £500	− £500	− £500	− £500
1	100	+ 91	87	85	85
2	200	+ 165	151	146	144
3	200	+ 150	131	125	122
4	200	+ 137	114	107	103
5	100	+ 62	50	46	44
		105	33	9	−2

If we use 15 per cent we get an NPV of £33. Moving up further to 17 per cent we get £9 and at 18 per cent −£2. In other words the DCF rate is just below 18 per cent. A figure of 17·8 per cent is probably sufficiently accurate for most purposes. With practice it is possible to arrive at a DCF rate quite quickly.

More Advanced DCF

In order to work out the DCF rate of return on any project it is necessary to make a number of preliminary calculations and assumptions to determine the cash flows. For instance the initial capital cost of the project is assessed. The running costs are based on assumptions about the price of raw materials and the level of other operating costs. Earnings are based on assumptions as to the price and level of sales of the project's final product.

Suppose some of these assumptions are wrong—almost certainly they will be. What is the effect on our DCF calculation? Not just the effect on the calculation, but the effect on the underlying profitability of our project.

For any large project it is essential to carry out a number of incremental DCF calculations. These are done to see what is the effect of variations in the assumptions. For instance calculations might be made to determine the effect of 10 per cent and 20 per cent increase and decrease in sales.

An examination of the resulting DCF rate will highlight the areas of risk and opportunity in the project. This in turn shows the Project Manager, if it is decided to proceed with the project, those areas which most need his attention to secure the profitability of the project. In some cases it may be shown that a 10 per cent variance—in, say, the cost of raw material—has only a marginal effect on the DCF rate. This may suggest a technical examination of the advantages to be gained from using a higher grade of raw material.

If a project is capable of being implemented in a number of phases, DCF calculations should be made for implementation based on a number of different timescales. Similarly where possible DCF calculations may well indicate that a particular self-contained part of a project should be dropped. If it is an essential part of the project, then it should be subjected to further technical examination to see whether an alternative and more profitable method can be found.

A company basically undertakes a project for profit. It is, therefore, interested in two aspects of profitability. The capital which is used for a project will be partly company money, or shareholders' equity, and partly borrowed money. The overall profitability as expressed by the project DCF rate is of importance in deciding whether to proceed with a project or not. However, the owners are also interested in the return to them, whether they are a family owning a small contracting business or the shareholders in a multinational mining corporation. The DCF rate of return on the equity capital, the owner's capital excluding borrowed money, should always be calculated as well.

Some firms are orientated to the view that the success of their activities can be judged by the return on the equity or owner's capital. They may be tempted to judge projects solely on the DCF rate of return on the equity. This can be dangerous. A highly geared project, one depending heavily on borrowed money, may show a healthy DCF return on the equity while the overall DCF rate gives only a marginally higher rate of return than the cost of borrowing. A project which goes ahead on this basis can be financially unstable. Quite apart from variations from the planned assumptions, there can be marked variations in interest rates over the life of a project.

214

If the return on the overall project falls below the rate of interest payable on the loans, this will result in loss. When earnings were positive the high proportion of borrowed money resulted in high return on equity capital.

With negative earnings the gearing works in the opposite direction, leading to a heavy loss to the owners of the equity.

DCF Traps

The theoretical basis on which the profitability of a project is calculated probably assumes an initial capital outlay followed by a period during which net earnings are received. Finally the net earnings ceases and the project is complete. This is shown in Fig. 16.4.

In practice life is not always as simple as that. There may be a significant negative cash flow at the end of the project. For instance in an open cast mining project there may be a requirement to return

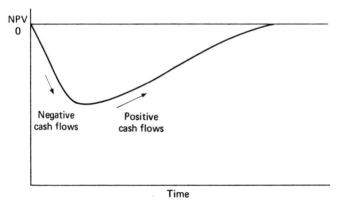

Fig. 16.4 Mining project cash flow

the mining area to its normal use on completion of the project. This may involve heavy capital expenditure on earthmoving, planting and landscaping. This expenditure occurs over an appreciable period of time and it is over a period during which there are no offsetting earnings.

Figure 16.5 illustrates the position. It shows the average capital employed on the project. This starts at zero and increases rapidly as

215

the initial capital is laid out. Then net earnings start to flow in. These earnings can be considered as partly the rate of return on the capital invested and partly as repayments of capital. The net earnings enable the cash flow to become positive and this process continues until NPV = 0 for the first time. It is then necessary to build up a capital sum to be used in returning the site to its natural state on completion of the mining operation where once again NPV = 0. This in turn brings an element of unrealism into the DCF calculation. Effectively, if the project DCF rate is, say, 15 per cent, then you are assuming that the money accumulated for the final project capital expenditure will earn 15 per cent while it is waiting to be used. This is, of course, improbable. Because the expenditure is fairly near at hand, the capital is probably accumulated in cash or cash deposit form, where it will earn a much lower rate of interest. This must be allowed for in the DCF calculation and a realistic fixed interest rate adopted for this period. For the sake of simplicity some large companies use a 0 per cent rate for this period.

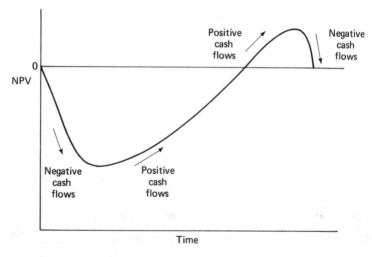

Fig. 16.5 Opencast mining project cash flow

seventeen The Price of Capital

Need for a Yardstick

No business can afford to pay more for its capital than it can earn on it. When stated boldly in this form it is a statement which few would dispute. Yet every year a great many firms go out of business because they are earning less on their capital than they have to pay for it. In most cases this is not done deliberately. A frequent cause is that the true price of capital has not been assessed.

Projects involve capital expenditure. Well planned projects are carefully evaluated to ensure that they are worthwhile. Much time and effort is expended in arriving at the NPV or DCF rate for the project. For very large projects large computers and a highly qualified staff may be employed for days, weeks or months evaluating the project with all its possible variations. They must have a yardstick against which to judge the project. It is the price of capital which provides this yardstick. As we shall see in a subsequent chapter other factors enter into the choice of projects. However, the price of capital is the basic yardstick, which can only be ignored at your peril.

We have seen that where the NPV (Net Present Value) of a project is calculated, it is necessary to assume a rate of return on capital. When the DCF rate is calculated, it is necessary to compare the result with something. Most organizations which are set up to handle projects have a yardstick rate of return. Straightforwardly this is the organization's price of capital. The actual rate used may in practice be higher than the calculated price of capital to allow for uncertainties in the calculation. Even the United Kingdom civil service recognizes that capital has a price. HM Treasury has a 'test discount rate' which is used for the appraisal of investment projects in the public sector.

Capital is a scarce resource and is likely to remain so for the indefinite future. Like every other resource, it has a price. At first sight it may seem easy to determine the price of capital—just take current bank rate or the rate of overdraft interest being charged by banks. Unfortunately it is not as easy as that. The price of capital varies continuously and varies from organization to organization. In 1970 in the United Kingdom it was possible for a small business man to pay an effective rate of interest of 25 per cent on a secured loan, while a large public company could borrow at $5\frac{1}{2}$ per cent to finance the export of goods to be used in an overseas project.

Sources of Capital

The rest of this chapter is given over to a consideration of the price of capital to a public company. Some of the principles do apply equally to the price of capital for public bodies, but in general special considerations apply to such bodies.

Basically companies obtain their capital by two means, firstly from shareholders and secondly by borrowing. There was a time when many people regarded borrowing money for either personal or business purposes as suspect or even slightly immoral. The pace of inflation in the years since the Second World War has produced a gradual change of opinion. Debt has become respectable. The advantages of gearing are now fully appreciated, though perhaps its dangers are overlooked. Indeed the advantages are now so clearly obvious to all that the price of borrowed money has risen markedly.

Shareholders' Capital

Shareholders fall broadly into two classes, preference shareholders and ordinary shareholders. In the United Kingdom, preference shares can be disregarded. They are shares issued at a fixed rate of interest. They do not participate in the profits of a company beyond their fixed rate of interest. Because they are shares, the interest on them is not chargeable before UK corporation tax becomes due. Hence in the UK they have become an expensive way of raising fixed interest capital. Although many companies still have preference shares in their capital structure, practically no new issues of preference shares are made. Many companies have redeemed their existing preference capital or have exchanged the shares for some other cheaper form of borrowing.

Ordinary (or equity) shareholders are the owners of a normal limited liability company. They contribute additional capital in one of two ways.

A company can make a new issue of ordinary shares. It is common to issue these slightly below the market value of the existing shares and offer them as 'rights' to existing shareholders. These shares may be issued on a yield basis of 4 per cent or even less. However as we shall see later the true cost of ordinary shares to a company is considerably more than the immediate dividend yield. If the company does not pay out its full profits in a year in the form of dividend, then the balance is effectively added to the capital of the company. This balance is known as the retained earnings. On the face of its it this is a cheap way to obtain fresh capital. However, the proportion of its profits which a company can retain is limited by the expectations of the shareholders. Also the shareholders expect at least as good a return from their profits left with a company as they could get by receiving them as dividends and investing the proceeds in some other company or in some form of loan.

The cost of the equity in a company is a study in itself. Those who are interested in the subject should consult one of the expert books by A. J. Merrett and Alan Sykes such as *Capital Budgeting and Company Finance*. Historically it would appear that equity shareholders require a return on their capital of 7 per cent a year in real terms net of all taxes. The cost of this depends on a number of factors such as the current rates of tax and the proportion of earnings paid out as dividends. Typically the cost of providing this 7 per cent return to a company might be 14 per cent in money terms on new issues of shares and $11\frac{1}{2}$ per cent in money terms on retained earnings. This return to ordinary shareholders is made up of both dividends and capital gains. Capital gains result from putting the retained earnings to work for the company, thus generating increased earnings for the company. The increased earnings result in an increase in share price. This is, of course, a grossly oversimplified view of the causes of share price movements. However it is generally true that

219

increased earnings per share lead to higher share prices. A return which takes the form of increased share value is attractive to many shareholders. It is not subject to income tax and surtax—unless the gain is realized by a sale of the shares within a year of their purchase. Normally, the shares being held for longer than this, the shareholder is only liable for capital gains tax at a maximum of 30 per cent. Furthermore the payment of this tax can effectively be deferred as it is only payable when the shares are sold.

The cost to a company of providing a given return to the shareholders is less in the case of funds provided from retained earnings than it is when the funds are raised by a new share issue. In the case we have already considered, this was $11\frac{1}{2}$ per cent against 14 per cent. This difference is due to the difference in tax treatment.

Borrowed Capital

Borrowing may take many forms. The most common are bank overdrafts and loans, issues of debentures and loan stocks, and mortgages on properties. The amount that can be borrowed depends upon the credit status of the borrower, the nature of his business, the proportion that existing loans are to equity capital and the proposed way in which the money will be used. The interest rate which will be charged is related to the same factors. It is also affected by the general level of interest rates and the anticipated length of time for which the money is required. The real cost of borrowed money during inflationary times is very much lower than it appears. Interest paid by a company on loans is 'tax deductable'. If inflation continues at $3\frac{1}{2}$ per cent a year, then £1000 borrowed in 1970 is paid back in 1990 with £1000 which in terms of 1970 purchasing power is worth only £500. The real value of the interest payments has also gone down year by year.

What is this price of capital for a particular project? How is it calculated? The first thing to determine is whether the cost of the capital to be raised for a project can be identified as particular to that project or whether it comes from the company's general supply of capital. Normally for small to medium sized projects it is not possible to identify which capital went into which project. Normal practice is, therefore, to calculate the average cost of new capital to the company and use this as the yardstick against which to judge all the firm's projects. Because a company raises different amounts of capital from various sources and at different rates of interest, it is normal to calculate the average on a basis weighted according to the source of capital. For example if £10,000 is raised at 10 per cent and £20,000 at 13 per cent the weighted average cost of capital is 12 per cent. The actual calculation is very much more complicated because of the effects of tax and inflation.

Special Cases

We have said that generally the cost of capital is the average of the cost of capital available to the company, weighted according to its source and cost. However, there are some cases where the capital to be used is clearly identified with the project. Such a case occurs where a property developer laboriously acquires a number of sites, which together form a site for a large office block. He lets the building on a long lease to a well established public company before he starts to build. In such circumstances the developer can borrow a very high proportion of the project cost on the security of the building. A similar case arises with large mining projects such as the Bougainville copper mine in the territory of Papua and New Guinea. For this project letters of intent were obtained from Japanese firms covering the supply of 950,000 tons of copper. These were subsequently made firm in contracts for over a million tons of copper to be delivered over a period of 15 years. A large part of the financing of the project was arranged in the form of loans. Loans of $246·4 million were arranged between the Bank of America and the Commonwealth Trading Bank. Mitsui and Co. and Mitsubishi Shoji Kaisha agreed to advance a further $30 million.

In cases like Bougainville it is sensible to calculate a price of capital for the particular project rather than take a company average. This also is the type of project with heavy loan financing, where a DCF calculation should be done on an equity basis. In this type of DCF calculation the loans, their interest and repayment are treated as cash flows and the DCF return is calculated on the equity capital. This DCF return is then compared against the company's price of equity capital.

221

An Essential Tool

The price of capital is an essential yardstick against which to measure the profitability of projects. In small concerns it is a figure constantly in the minds of the management. In large organizations it is a figure which should be published to Project Managers and planners. The price of capital is not just an esoteric figure to be considered by company directors and calculated by their accountants. It is a tool of project management. Project Managers must be concerned not only with the execution of their projects but also with their profitability.

In the narrow view, it is in the Project Manager's interest to run a successful and profitable project. For him it should result in salary increases, bonuses, continuity of employment and an enhanced reputation. It is also important to the company for which he works. A company whose projects are profitable can expand and bring useful, satisfying and rewarding work to the whole body of its employees. The prosperity of whole villages and towns may reflect the profitability of large projects. Profitable projects at home and overseas contribute to the expansion of the national product and to the national wellbeing.

In order to tell whether a project is profitable you require a yardstick against which to measure it. That yardstick is the price of capital.

eighteen Project Choice

Is it only Money?

We have seen how the financial appraisal of projects is carried out in modern firms. But is project choice merely a matter of listing net present values or DCF rates and choosing the project with the highest figure?

The answer, most emphatically, is 'No.' Project choice is and probably always will be a matter of judgement. Working out the DCF rates of return or the net present values can be delegated to junior staff. The final decision is based on management's judgement.

The object of this chapter is to consider how management can successfully exercise its judgement in the selection of projects. Project selection is not a mere passive matter of evaluating the projects which are offered. Opportunities must be recognized. The project orientated company must take positive action to find the projects which will use its resources to the greatest effect. Each project must be seen both as a profitable enterprise in its own right and also as a bridge into the future.

The process of project selection may be considered logically under the following headings:

The inventory of resources.
The management framework.
The detailed evaluation.
Recognizing the opportunities.

The Inventory of Resources

In the Stock Exchange there is a saying 'cut your losses and run your profits'. In the armed forces an acknowledged basic principle is to 'reinforce success'. In selecting projects, management must find those which will enable the firm to make the fullest use of its strengths. This does not mean that you should always undertake those projects which are the same as last time. In the environment in which we live this is a sure prescription for eventual failure. Existing strengths must be used to build for the future. The first step is, therefore, to take stock of our strengths, in fact to make an inventory of our resources.

Broadly an organization's resources are material, financial and human. Material resources cover property, stocks, rights of various kinds, tools and capital equipment. Where an organization is short of material resources it can generally, given adequate financial resources, buy what it needs in terms of material. However there are some material resources which give particular strength to an organization. These include the material rights which protect existing knowhow—copyright and patent rights. Certain rights over property can also be a great strength and can be exploited in the organization's project programme. There are some items of capital equipment which are expensive and which have a long gestation period from initial order or conception to delivery. The possession of such an item may give a commanding position in a particular field.

Financial resources are of considerable importance. A strong financial position can be exploited to seize opportunities denied to your financially weaker rivals. Financial weakness can limit the possibilities which can be considered. However, in the long run financial resources will flow to the organizations which are seen to be successful and profitable. Money will flow to the organization which has good human resources effectively deployed and well managed.

The real strength of any organization lies in its human resources—in its people. A successful project orientated organization depends upon a variety of human skills. Management and technical skills are the most obvious. Your organization may be fortunate in having people with a particular flair, a financial wizard or a man who knows

224

his way thoroughly through a particular branch of the law. These particular human strengths may take many forms from people with creativity and special insight to the person with good contacts.

There are some strengths which in effect are derived from a mixture of the basic material, financial and human resources. A distribution network, an effective research laboratory or a strong Development Department can be a source of great strength. Goodwill or reciprocal trading arrangements are strengths which can open up project possibilities.

Whatever the strengths of an organization may be, they should be identified and known to management. The extent to which they are fully used or are capable of further use must be established. When these resources will become free for use on future projects must also be forecast.

When you have identified the strengths of your organization, when you have an inventory of your resources, you have taken the first step towards successful project selection.

Although it is a first step it is a continuing one. Your inventory of resources must be kept continually up to date. This may be done in many ways. In a very small organization, it may all be carried in one man's head. In a very big one it may be in a computer maintained data base.

The Management Framework

In small organizations, the whole process of project selection is probably handled informally by the owner or top manager. In large organizations it is necessary to delegate much of the work.

The preliminary work of investigating projects costs money and may indeed be very costly. It is essential that the people engaged on this work do not waste their efforts on projects which the organization will never follow up. It is equally important to drop investigations into projects as soon as it is clear that they cannot be viable. To make this possible management must have formulated its aims and set them out sufficiently clearly for the project planners to plan on them. A project should never reach board level for decision on the go ahead only to be thrown out because it is at variance with the organization's aims. If it does there is something wrong with the way in which management has formulated and communicated its aims.

Management must try to set as objective a framework as possible for project selection. There is always a danger in large organizations that the internal politics of the organization will affect the outcome of project selection procedures. Another danger is that in reaching the stage of becoming a project for serious consideration, a proposed project may develop a momentum of its own. To the project's backers it becomes a matter of prestige that it should go forward. The project selection and review procedure must be designed to minimize these dangers.

The target rate of return on investment is an important part of the management aim. The way in which the target rate is handled varies. Sometimes it is a single minimum rate to be achieved on all investment. Sometimes effectively it is a scale of rates against risks with a lower rate for a virtually risk free project than for more normal projects.

Very small companies, where the controlling entrepreneur carries the aims of the company in his head, can succeed. Large organizations will only bumble along, with the occasional stumble, unless they formulate their aims clearly and communicate them effectively to their planning staff.

The Detailed Evaluation

A project may start as an idea which is discussed by the planning staff thrown up by one of the organization's managers or suggested from outside. If, on the face of it, it is a project in line with the organization's aims and with possibilities it should go forward for detailed evaluation.

The detailed evaluation must be soundly based on:

Reliable and accurate information.
Where full information is not available, and it very rarely is, on credible assumptions.
The use of sound techniques to evaluate the information and assumptions.
Evaluation of the resources required and the extent to which they will be available.
Continuous review.

The first stage of the evaluation is probably a project appreciation.

In this the main aspects of the project are committed to paper. The background to the proposed project is set down with a statement showing how it will benefit the organization. A project aim is stated. All the factors likely to affect the project are set down briefly. The main possible ways of tackling the project are described with their advantages and disadvantages. Finally, a recommendation is made for the continuing evaluation of the project and an outline of the method of execution of the project to be adopted if the project goes forward.

Management can make a decision on whether to go forward with the project evaluation on the basis of this initial project appreciation.

RELIABLE AND ACCURATE INFORMATION

Project evaluation is what is known as an iterative process. That is to say a decision is not made once and for all. In the early stages of project evaluation only some of the information needed for planning is available. The rest is a fog of uncertainty. A complete picture or model of the project is built up, covering the project from start to finish. The first picture may well be built up on very few facts. As more facts become available so the picture is modified. The original basic facts may be the grade of mineral ore at a given location, the size of the population of a certain area or the rate of production possible with a particular machine. A whole pyramid of assumptions and calculations may be built up on these few basic facts. The answer at the end may be calculated to six places of decimals, but if the facts fed in at the beginning of the process were nonsense, the answer at the end is likely to be nonsense as well. It is essential to check and cross check the facts. As the investigation of a project proceeds every opportunity should be taken to check that the initial facts are correct. For example, the yield of an ore body may be based on limited bore hole results. Further drilling may indicate that the initial information, while correct so far as it went, was not typical of the whole ore body.

THE ASSUMPTIONS

Almost more important than the basic facts are the assumptions made. No one can know for certain the trend of prices and sales over a period of several years ahead. Worse still no one can predict with accuracy the future actions and attitudes of governments—in particular how they will act in tax matters and in giving differential encouragement to investment.

The most important assumptions in many projects are the amount of final product which can be sold, the price at which it can be sold and the phasing of the sales. This is as true of a speculative estate of dwelling houses put up by a small local builder as it is of a new multi-million pound copper mine being considered by a mining finance house. In such projects the greater the degree of certainty about the final marketing operation, the easier it will be both to finance the operation with additional loans and also to decide on whether to go ahead with the project. When the facts come to be studied these items may appear so critical that a further investigation is needed. A market survey may be carried out or in an extreme case consultants may be called in to give an independent opinion. A firm may be committed to a project which it has to complete to a fixed time and price, for instance the construction of a section of motorway or a turnkey computer project. Here the key assumptions are likely to be those relating to time. Are the requirements clear enough to permit work to start? What assumptions have been made about the speed with which the necessary resources can be mobilized? The probability of all these time assumptions must be carefully considered.

SOUND TECHNIQUES

The techniques by which project planning information may be evaluated have been referred to elsewhere in this book. The financial evaluation will have been carried out using DCF and NPV techniques. The time and resource facts and assumptions will have been evaluated using PERT. There is nothing very clever about the techniques themselves but they do permit a sound evaluation of a mass of facts and assumptions.

These techniques will be applied not just to the most probable facts and assumptions. A whole range of possibilities will be evaluated in order to highlight the risks and opportunities.

In this careful procedure of project evaluation, there is the danger of the evaluation taking so long that the opportunity is missed. This is a particular danger in the large bureaucratically controlled organization.

RESOURCES

An essential part of the evaluation is to calculate the phased resource requirements of the project. Work must then be done to see whether the resources will be available within the organization. If they will not, can the project be rephased so as to fit in with what resources will be available? The possibility of reallocating resources from other work must be considered together with the implications of such reallocation. The possibility of obtaining additional resources from outside the organization must be considered. One of the prime concerns of management is the allocation of scarce resources. It is also a key factor in project selection.

CONTINUOUS REVIEW

Some people think that a decision is made once and finished with. This may be so in some military or crisis situations. But in project work decision making is a continuous process. Even to consider a large project costs money. At the minimum staff are tied up for a period in making calculations and preparing a plan. At a maximum, surveys may be carried out; for a building or mining project bore holes may be sunk; outside professional work may be commissioned. In all sorts of ways money and effort may be spent over several months and years before the point of no return is finally reached.

Throughout this period the calculations and assumptions must be continually reviewed and at planned intervals the decision to go ahead and incur further expenditure must be consciously reviewed.

Recognizing the Opportunities

Perhaps illogically, we have left this aspect of project selection to the last. In any project orientated company there will be a regular flow of project proposals from many sources. However, as well as earning current profits a company is concerned to use its present strengths to build for the future.

In saying that we should select projects which will help us forward in the future, we are not advocating that unprofitable or prestige projects should be undertaken. In any organization there will always be those who advocate the taking on of such projects. Sales management seems particularly fascinated by prestigious new frontier projects. In most cases it just is not worth going in for such projects unless they will also show a satisfactory profit. Should it be decided that it is necessary to undertake a project in a particular field, then at least the implications should be as fully calculated as possible. Has the best available project been selected from those available? Could some effort result in a better project prospect being created? Does the project really build on existing strengths or is it a leap in the dark? There must be a careful analysis of what will be gained from taking on the project and what will be the cost—not only direct costs but the cost of profitable opportunities foregone. We believe that by thorough forward planning and careful project selection over the years it should be possible to build one's bridges into the future without indulging in profitless prestige projects.

One way of building these bridges into the future is to use special projects as a test bed for future standard products.

The greatest opportunities arise from the recognition of new trends. A successful company makes a conscious effort to collect project ideas from among its own staff. It must also be conscious of what is going on in the world outside. At a minimum the activities of rivals in the same field at home and abroad should be monitored. The trade press must be studied and contacts with individuals and organizations engaged in research must be cultivated.

However, a development outside a firm's normal field may often provide the greatest opportunities. It is the characteristic of the effective entrepreneur that he recognizes these opportunities. The limitation of many large organizations is that their managers are good administrators rather than entrepreneurs. They do not recognize the opportunities, which go by default.

Do Profits Matter?

We started this chapter by asking, 'Is it only money?' We gave the answer, 'No'.

However, even though money is not the be all and end all of project selection, we must not forget that profits do matter. An organization may survive an occasional loss making project. In the end a project orientated organization will only survive and prosper if its projects are profitable. One of the most important factors leading to profitable projects is the careful and methodical search for and selection of the right projects for the organization.

230

Successful project selection above all depends on the correct evaluation of the organization's human resources and matching them to those projects where they can be deployed to the maximum effect.

part five Further Project
Considerations

nineteen Some Miscellaneous Commercial Considerations

IT IS POSSIBLE TO bring a project to a conclusion successfully in the sense that a bridge, an oil refinery or a computer installation is completed to specification, or an open cast mine is brought into production. It may be unsuccessful in the wider sense because it fails to make a profit. In a commercial organization this is failure. Nowadays, even government sponsored projects are expected to show a profit in some sense. Without profit, capital for future projects is not forthcoming.

A group of factors, which make for success or failure of a project in the wider sense, can be grouped under the title miscellaneous commercial factors. Wide awake organizations take these factors into account when they evaluate potential projects. The commercial situation is a continuously changing one. It must be sized up afresh for each new project and kept under review during the life of the project.

Tax

The first commercial factor to consider is tax. What taxes will affect your project? How can these taxes be mitigated?

Tax is far too complicated and fast changing a subject to be dealt with in a book of this nature. Good professional advice on the subject must be taken. All we can do is to illustrate the importance of the subject. Rules as to how capital investment is treated for tax purposes vary. It may be possible to treat some expenditure as

234

current expenditure chargeable against current income from other projects of the same organization, thus reducing current taxation. Some countries, which wish to encourage exploration for and exploitation of, raw material resources allow particularly favourable treatment—sometimes even granting tax holidays for a period.

The timing of tax payments and rebates is of particular importance in the DCF calculations for a project and frequently makes the difference between a project being accepted or rejected.

Government Grants

Allied to the subject of tax is that of grants from the government. These may be made by governments of industrial countries to projects which will bring work to poor, backward or run down areas of the country. These can be of great importance and it may well be worth organizing the project in discrete stages to obtain such grants as each stage is completed.

Government Assistance

Governments from time to time are keen to encourage certain activities. Where a project involves developing a mine or building an oil refinery or aluminium smelter in a remote part of the country, Government assistance may be obtainable. Sometimes this is available as a matter of routine. At other times or for particular forms of assistance, it may be necessary to do some lobbying or special pleading. Assistance may take the form of provision of infrastructure —building of roads, docks or airfields. It may involve nationalized industries giving special terms for power. Local authorities may provide housing for key project staff.

UK Government assistance may take the form of insurance of some risks through the Export Credit Guarantee Department. For instance if a railway is to be built overseas and the initial rolling stock is provided as part of the project, ECGD cover can be obtained for value of the exports from the UK.

An example of the way in which ECGD guarantees can be of help is the Ultramar Quebec oil refinery project. In January 1969 Ultramar had net assets of only £31,800,000 against which it had loans outstanding of over £14 million. Despite this Ultramar was able to borrow more than £23 million against the total planned cost of £27 million for its Quebec refinery project. Ultramar was able to do this in part at least because it was able to get an ECGD guarantee to cover the export of some £14 million worth of UK supplied equipment for use in the construction of the refinery. Furthermore with government encouragement the UK banks gave loans at a preferential rate of interest. Ultramar were able to obtain a £14 million loan from UK banks at a rate of interest of $5\frac{1}{2}$ per cent, well below the open market rate at the time. On top of the assistance from the UK Government and banks, Ultramar was able to plan on receiving grants of £2·14 million from the Canadian and Quebec provincial Governments, to be paid on completion of the project.

Government assistance overseas can be indirect. Where contracts for large projects are awarded by international organizations, it is common for governments to lobby on behalf of their nationals. Governments may want to see their country's influence in a particular area extended and will make considerable efforts on behalf of their nationals both to help get the contract for the project in the first place, in advising about local conditions and in helping to smooth out local difficulties.

Customs Duties

If a project is being undertaken on behalf of a government or a multi-national organization, it may be possible to import equipment and stores free of customs and excise duties. In the United Kingdom, if equipment is imported with a view to work being done on it for subsequent shipment overseas, it is possible to claim repayment of customs duties on final re-export. This is known as customs drawback.

Restraints on Trade

There are a number of restraints on trade between countries including in some cases absolute embargoes. For instance at various times the UK and USA Governments have banned the export of goods of strategic importance to the USSR, China and Eastern

Europe. Any project to be executed in these countries needs careful checking to ensure that no equipment vital to the project will be embargoed.

Similarly from time to time the United Nations may impose sanctions against a country such as those imposed on Rhodesia.

The Arab States have from time to time imposed embargoes on Israeli goods and services. They have even gone further and attempted to embargo foreign firms known to trade with Israel.

This may sound of very little concern to the Project Manager. But the problems are real for the manager of a construction project in the Middle East or the manager who is trying to provide a factory on a turnkey basis in the USSR. Even if they do not occur on this scale it is almost certain that a project of any size will be affected at some stage by government restriction or regulation. When executing a project in your own country in your normal line of business, these restrictions are probably so well known to you and your firm that they are taken as a matter or routine. When operating overseas or in fresh territory it is worth exploring the position before becoming too deeply involved. If at a late stage in the project you find that a key item is embargoed, it may become at best more expensive and take longer to complete the project. At worst completion may become impossible.

Currency Restrictions

Many countries from time to time put restrictions on the convertibility of their currencies. This can affect a project in several ways. First payment for a project or profits from the operation of an overseas project may be frozen in the foreign currency in which they are paid. You may even find yourself in a barter situation, where the price paid for your project is cocoa, steel, glass or oil.

If some of the equipment for a project is to be bought from a foreign country, provision has to be made to obtain the necessary foreign currency. For equipment ordered well in advance of delivery, the possibility of hedging the currency risk should be considered. The possibility of devaluation should always be covered in any contract involving foreign currency. Any remaining risk can then be insured against, directly or indirectly.

Business Ethics

Business ethics vary from country to country. In the UK the standard of business ethics is high and bribery is probably exceptional in helping to produce a contract or in finding ways around Government regulations. However, even in the UK judicious cultivation of the right people can help. Entertainment and all expenses paid, visits to similar projects already in operation can be instrumental in smoothing out difficulties.

In some countries bribes or tips are an accepted part of life. Where this is neglected, goods will be delayed in customs; forms will get lost between government offices and it will become impossible to see the officials whose help you need. In these circumstances, it is necessary to discover with all speed what the local custom is and who are the people who can help. A cynic once said that every man has his price. Remember that the price may not always be a money one.

Commodity Price Fluctuations

Commodity prices can affect a project's profitability. A project involving the supply of heavy electrical equipment may require a significant quantity of copper. The price of copper fluctuates over a wide range and in the course of a year may vary by as much as £200 a ton. Hence the copper for the project should be purchased for later delivery at the time the contract for the project is entered into.

Commodity price fluctuations have a much greater impact on projects whose purpose is the final production of a commodity. For instance several years may elapse between planning an iron mine and the first delivery of iron ore or pellets. In the course of planning the project it will be wise to try to line up contracts for the sale of at least a proportion of the mine's production for a number of years ahead. Done successfully this provides a guaranteed minimum income from the project. It may also provide additional security for borrowing. In these circumstances, it may become possible to borrow an abnormally high proportion of the cost of the project at interest rates which are not completely prohibitive. The Rio Tinto Zinc Corporation is a past master at this. Their Hamersley Iron Ore subsidiary in Western Australia for instance is a highly geared operation. Much of the finance for the project was raised at a very early stage on the strength of letters of intent from seven Japanese steel companies. These letters covered sales of over 65 million tons of ore to be delivered over 15 years.

Commercial Opportunities

These commercial considerations should not depress you. They are a source of opportunity for the wide awake organization. In a large firm, the corporate planning organization will keep tax and trade considerations under review. For smaller firms the first place to turn for advice may well be the bank. Most banks, through their network of branches and correspondents are in a position to advise about conditions in foreign countries. Similarly, the Board of Trade has a number of advisory services and is particularly keen to help UK firms in any way which will increase UK exports.

In fact much valuable commercial information is freely available in the newspapers and magazines such as the *Economist*. The ways in which this information is turned to benefit in bringing about profitable projects is essentially simple. Unfortunately many organizations and project teams fail to look at all at the commercial angles, and hence many projects which could be profitable are discarded. The successful Project Manager ensures that all the angles are studied.

239

twenty The Computer as a Tool of Project Management

Introduction

One thing that Project Managers need to do is to familiarize themselves with the tools they can have at their disposal to save time or to perform a task more accurately. The computer is undoubtedly such a tool, and while Project Managers cannot all be computer experts they can find out how to benefit their project using either a bureau machine or their own company computer.

PERT (TIME)

There are several advantages in using computer PERT in the project:

On any project with more than a few hundred activities with frequent (fortnightly) updating, the cost of the computer will usually be equal to, or not much more than, the cost of manual methods. Any extra cost will be more than made up by the speed, accuracy and facilities of the computer.

There are facilities normally built into computer PERT packages which are available without extra effort, e.g. many forms of printouts, bar charts, etc. To do the same thing by hand is very laborious and less error free.

The PERT network and its updated information is held in a backing store (usually magnetic tape or disc) and there is minimum risk of unofficial alteration or corruption. Manual methods are always suspect in this respect with changes being carried out and not recorded.

Once the network and accompanying information is incorporated into the computer storage, changes can be quickly carried out and new printouts produced. Since there is always a discipline involved in doing this, it is rare to find uncorrected issue numbers on updated information. In connection with the general subject of updating, speed and accuracy are essential, otherwise the new information is already out of date in a quickly moving project.

Another very useful thing about the computer printouts is that if they can be accepted by all of the contributors to the project then a more uniform communication comes about. The 'paper under the desk' disappears and everyone speaks the same language. There is one control document that everyone can see and deal with.

Finally, and in perhaps a more qualitative sense, the work on PERT in updating and calculation is tedious. While the theory is that one is comparing computer costs with lower grade labour costs, this is not always the case; higher grade labour may have to do the work because the lower grade labour just does not exist. In any case supervision and checking of the manual process will be necessary.

The type of information that can be obtained via the computer output is large. Among the most common are:

> All activities with and without dummy activities and/or completed activities.
> Activities scheduled to fall in the next time period of choice.
> Key activities only.
> Critical activities only.
> All events.
> Key events.
> Specified events.
> Activities in total float order.
> Activities by department.
> Bar charts of various types, etc., etc.

All these are obtained with no more human effort than for one output.

INPUT DATA

The user usually has two choices either to prepare the input data in a form suitable for direct input into a computer or let a bureau prepare it direct from the PERT chart. This latter may be the easier course and the cost may not exceed about twice the cost of in house preparation. In the case of computer owners it is almost certain they will have their own data preparation facilities.

The general instructions for input data cover:

Parameter data, i.e.:
    Printout information required.
Project number or reference.
    Project description.
Activity codes, i.e.:
    Cost centre.
    Responsible organization for an activity.
Type of trade or work.
Activity information, i.e.:
    Description.
    Activity code.
    Activity number.
    Preceding and succeeding events.

Project Appraisal, Costs and Accounting

There are two major aspects of this both admirably suited to computer operation, e.g. long, tedious, repetitive but fairly standardized arithmetic.

There is the appraisal of the project in the first instance in terms of a financial evaluation. We have shown in previous chapters how the traditional evaluation techniques, involving average yearly rates and payback periods have serious limitations and how the discounted cash flow techniques offer a much more realistic evaluation of cost and profitability. The computer can calculate DCF rates for the project under varying simulated times, progress, capital costs and revenue. A judgement can then be made as to the worth of one project against another in terms of the financial effects. We can then go further into the provision of project or company models.

What should come out of such a model? As with all management information, the level of it must be appropriate to the user and might vary from sales volume statistics, changes in sales price, to cash flows, profit rating, key ratios or rates of growth.

A project or company model will go through many phases in the processing and analysis of data. Firstly a picture is built up from the known data. Dependent upon the type of project or company it is likely to include:

Market information, e.g. sales volume, prices.
Production information, e.g. costs, lead times.
Financial information, e.g. cash flows, discount rates.
Key ratios, e.g. turnover per employee.

Secondly this model provides facilities for varying all or some of the key items, e.g. share of total market trends, seasonal variations, investment incentives, cash grants, initial allowances, annuities and overdrafts. Thereafter, the financial effects of these variations are used to enable a continuous appraisal of the project to take place. In this appraisal management must assess the profitability and risks on the basis of the results produced from the computer based model.

The computer can also provide the normal accounting functions and these probably form a large part of present computer utilization. The organization of such accounting procedures is relatively simple and budgets, expenditure and variances should be regularly provided to the project.
PERT cost techniques can be used for more specialized cost control.

Scientific Calculations

This is a commonplace use of computers but even so is not used as fully as it might be by many companies. Apart from the types of calculations dealing with specific subjects likely in various projects, e.g. beam stresses, concrete load factors, electronic circuit analysis, etc. there are more general mathematical techniques. These include linear programming, matrix schemes and statistical analysis.

The moral for Project Managers is that it is almost certain that a computer program package will exist which would help solve problems in a particular project.

Management Information Services

While the Project Manager can obtain PERT and project costs from

243

computer outputs there is still a very large amount of project information that, if more rapidly available, would be of tremendous assistance. The problem is twofold:

> Project information is usually spread over too many people or it is written and contained on too many pieces of paper.
> The time to seek out information is too long.

As the Project Manager succeeds in controlling the project by the use of sound preparatory, analysis and control techniques the need to improve the system is always pressing. The pressure arises not only from the project complexity growth, customer timescale reductions and other project factors, but from the necessity to explore all aspects of the project in greater depth than before. This is going to mean large storage of data in data banks or data bases.

These terms cover a multitude of procedures and information storage that the Project Manager will certainly use increasingly. Over the next 10 to 15 years more and more of these data banks will be set up either in centres or in companies. The full benefit will, of course, not be felt without the accompanying keyboard terminals. With these the Project Manager will be able to access the bank and either update or interrogate. Such items as PERT, cost analysis, calculations and accounting are now readily available and more will follow. There is not the slightest doubt that as projects become more and more complex in their organization and technology, the data base will enable the Project Manager to manage with the necessary detailed information he will require.

Appendix Discount Tables

YEAR (n)

r%	¼	½	1	2	3	4	5	6	7	8	9	10	11	12	13	14	15	16
½	9988	9975	9950	9901	9851	9802	9754	9705	9657	9609	9561	9513	9466	9419	9372	9326	9279	923
1	9975	9950	9901	9803	9706	9610	9515	9420	9327	9235	9143	9053	8963	8874	8787	8700	8613	852
2	9950	9901	9804	9612	9423	9238	9057	8880	8706	8535	8368	8203	8043	7885	7730	7579	7430	728
3	9927	9853	9709	9426	9151	8885	8626	8375	8131	7894	7664	7441	7224	7014	6810	6611	6419	623
4	9902	9806	9615	9246	8890	8548	8219	7903	7599	7307	7026	6756	6496	6246	6006	5775	5553	533
5	9878	9759	9524	9070	8638	8227	7835	7462	7107	6768	6446	6139	5847	5568	5303	5051	4810	458
6	9855	9713	9434	8900	8396	7921	7473	7050	6651	6274	5919	5584	5268	4970	4688	4423	4173	393
7	9832	9667	9346	8734	8163	7629	7130	6663	6227	5820	5439	5083	4751	4440	4150	3878	3624	338
8	9810	9623	9259	8573	7938	7350	6806	6302	5835	5403	5002	4632	4289	3971	3677	3405	3152	291
9	9787	9579	9174	8417	7722	7084	6499	5963	5470	5019	4604	4224	3875	3555	3262	2992	2745	251
10	9765	9535	9091	8264	7513	6830	6209	5645	5132	4665	4241	3855	3505	3186	2897	2633	2394	217
11	9742	9491	9009	8116	7312	6587	5935	5346	4817	4339	3909	3522	3173	2858	2575	2320	2090	188
12	9721	9449	8929	7972	7118	6355	5674	5066	4523	4039	3606	3220	2875	2567	2292	2046	1827	163
13	9699	9407	8850	7831	6931	6133	5428	4803	4251	3762	3329	2946	2607	2307	2042	1807	1599	141
14	9678	9366	8772	7695	6750	5921	5194	4556	3996	3506	3075	2697	2366	2076	1821	1597	1401	122
15	9656	9325	8696	7561	6575	5718	4972	4323	3759	3269	2843	2472	2149	1869	1625	1413	1229	106
16	9636	9285	8621	7432	6407	5523	4761	4104	3538	3050	2630	2267	1954	1685	1452	1252	1079	093
17	9615	9245	8547	7305	6244	5337	4561	3898	3332	2848	2434	2080	1778	1520	1299	1110	0949	081
18	9594	9206	8475	7182	6086	5158	4371	3704	3139	2660	2255	1911	1619	1372	1163	0985	0835	070
19	9574	9167	8403	7062	5934	4987	4190	3521	2959	2487	2090	1756	1476	1240	1042	0876	0736	061
20	9555	9129	8333	6944	5787	4823	4019	3349	2791	2326	1938	1615	1346	1122	0935	0779	0649	054
21	9535	9091	8264	6830	5645	4665	3855	3186	2633	2176	1799	1486	1228	1015	0839	0693	0573	047
22	9515	9054	8197	6719	5507	4514	3700	3033	2486	2038	1670	1369	1122	0920	0754	0618	0507	041
23	9496	9016	8130	6610	5374	4369	3552	2888	2348	1909	1551	1262	1026	0834	0678	0551	0448	036
24	9476	8980	8065	6504	5245	4230	3411	2751	2218	1789	1443	1164	0938	0757	0610	0492	0397	032
25	9457	8945	8000	6400	5120	4096	3277	2621	2097	1678	1342	1074	0859	0687	0550	0440	0352	028
26	9438	8909	7937	6299	4999	3968	3149	2499	1983	1574	1249	0992	0787	0625	0496	0393	0312	024
27	9420	8874	7874	6200	4882	3844	3027	2383	1877	1478	1164	0916	0721	0568	0447	0352	0277	021
28	9401	8839	7813	6104	4768	3725	2910	2274	1776	1388	1084	0847	0662	0517	0404	0316	0247	019
29	9384	8804	7752	6009	4658	3611	2799	2170	1682	1304	1011	0784	0607	0471	0365	0283	0219	017
30	9365	8770	7692	5917	4552	3501	2693	2072	1594	1226	0943	0725	0558	0429	0330	0254	0195	015
35	9277	8607	7407	5487	4064	3011	2230	1652	1224	0906	0671	0497	0368	0273	0202	0150	0111	008
40	9193	8452	7143	5102	3644	2603	1859	1328	0949	0678	0484	0346	0247	0176	0126	0090	0064	004
45	9113	8305	6897	4756	3280	2262	1560	1076	0742	0512	0353	0243	0168	0116	0080	0055	0038	002
50	9036	8165	6667	4444	2963	1975	1317	0878	0585	0390	0260	0173	0116	0077	0051	0034	0023	001
r%	¼	½	1	2	3	4	5	6	7	8	9	10	11	12	13	14	15	16

YEAR

For the present value of £1 received in *n* years time. All figures are after the decimal point.

Example: Present value of £1 received in 9 years time = £0·9561
if discounted at ½ per cent a year
Present value of £1 received in 9 years time
if discounted at 8 per cent a year = £0·5002

YEAR (n)

17	18	19	20	21	22	23	24	25	26	27	28	29	30	35	40	45	50	r%
87	9141	9096	9051	9006	8961	8916	8872	8828	8784	8740	8697	8653	8610	8398	8191	7990	7793	½
444	8360	8277	8195	8114	8034	7954	7876	7798	7720	7644	7568	7493	7419	7059	6717	6391	6080	1
142	7002	6864	6730	6598	6468	6342	6217	6095	5976	5859	5744	5631	5521	5000	4529	4102	3715	2
050	5874	5703	5537	5375	5219	5067	4919	4776	4637	4502	4371	4243	4120	3554	3066	2644	2281	3
134	4936	4746	4564	4388	4220	4057	3901	3751	3607	3468	3335	3207	3083	2534	2083	1712	1407	4
363	4155	3957	3769	3589	3418	3256	3101	2953	2812	2678	2551	2429	2314	1813	1420	1113	0872	5
714	3503	3305	3118	2942	2775	2618	2470	2330	2198	2074	1956	1846	1741	1301	0972	0727	0543	6
166	2959	2765	2584	2415	2257	2109	1971	1842	1722	1609	1504	1406	1314	0937	0668	0476	0339	7
703	2502	2317	2145	1987	1839	1703	1577	1460	1352	1252	1159	1073	0994	0676	0460	0313	0213	8
311	2120	1945	1784	1637	1502	1378	1264	1160	1064	0976	0895	0822	0754	0490	0318	0207	0134	9
978	1799	1635	1486	1351	1228	1117	1015	0923	0839	0763	0693	0630	0573	0356	0221	0137	0085	10
696	1528	1377	1240	1117	1007	0907	0817	0736	0663	0597	0538	0485	0437	0259	0154	0091	0054	11
456	1300	1161	1037	0926	0826	0738	0659	0588	0525	0469	0419	0374	0334	0189	0107	0061	0035	12
252	1108	0981	0868	0768	0680	0601	0532	0471	0417	0369	0326	0289	0256	0139	0075	0041	0022	13
078	0946	0829	0728	0638	0560	0491	0431	0378	0331	0291	0255	0224	0196	0102	0053	0027	0014	14
929	0808	0703	0611	0531	0462	0402	0349	0304	0264	0230	0200	0174	0151	0075	0037	0019	0009	15
302	0691	0596	0514	0443	0382	0329	0284	0245	0211	0182	0157	0135	0116	0055	0026	0013	0006	16
693	0592	0506	0433	0370	0316	0270	0231	0197	0169	0144	0123	0105	0090	0041	0019	0009	0004	17
600	0508	0431	0365	0309	0262	0222	0188	0160	0135	0115	0097	0082	0070	0030	0013	0006	0003	18
520	0437	0367	0308	0259	0218	0183	0154	0129	0109	0091	0077	0064	0054	0023	0010	0004	0002	19
451	0376	0313	0261	0217	0181	0151	0126	0105	0087	0073	0061	0051	0042	0017	0007	0003	000	20
391	0323	0267	0221	0183	0151	0125	0103	0085	0070	0058	0048	0040	0033	0013	0005	0002	0001	21
340	0279	0229	0187	0154	0126	0103	0085	0069	0057	0047	0038	0031	0026	0009	0004	0001	0000	22
296	0241	0196	0159	0129	0105	0086	0070	0057	0046	0037	0030	0025	0020	0007	0003	0001	0000	23
258	0208	0168	0135	0109	0088	0071	0057	0046	0037	0030	0024	0020	0016	0005	0002	0001	0000	24
225	0180	0144	0115	0092	0074	0059	0047	0038	0030	0024	0019	0015	0012	0004	0001	0000		25
197	0156	0124	0098	0078	0062	0049	0039	0031	0025	0020	0015	0012	0010	0003	0001	0000		26
172	0135	0107	0084	0066	0052	0041	0032	0025	0020	0016	0012	0010	0008	0002	0001	0000		27
150	0118	0092	0072	0056	0044	0034	0027	0021	0016	0013	0010	0008	0006	0002	0001	0000		28
132	0102	0079	0061	0048	0037	0029	0022	0017	0013	0010	0008	0006	0005	0001	0000			29
116	0089	0068	0053	0040	0031	0024	0018	0014	0011	0008	0006	0005	0004	0001	0000			30
061	0045	0033	0025	0018	0014	0010	0007	0006	0004	0003	0002	0002	0001	0000				35
033	0023	0017	0012	0009	0006	0004	0003	0002	0002	0001	0001	0001	0000					40
018	0012	0009	0006	0004	0003	0002	0001	0001	0001	0000	0000	0000						45
010	0007	0005	0003	0002	0001	0001	0001	0000	0000									50

| 17 | 18 | 19 | 20 | 21 | 22 | 23 | 24 | 25 | 26 | 27 | 28 | 29 | 30 | 35 | 40 | 45 | 50 | r% |

YEAR

Bibliography

KINGSHOTT, A. L., *Investment Appraisal.* Ford Business Library. Published by Ford Motor Co. Ltd., 1967.

MERRETT, A. J. and SYKES, ALAN, *Capital Budgeting and Company Finance.* Published by Longmans, Green & Co., 1966.

JONES, H., *The Mathematics of Money.* Published by Blackie & Son, 1965.

ALFRED, A. M., *Discounted Cash Flow and Corporate Planning.* Woolwich Economic Papers, 1965.

HERTZ, DAVID B., 'Risk analysis in capital investment'. *Harvard Business Review,* Jan.– Feb., 1964.

ROCKLEY, L. E., *Capital Investment Decisisions.* Business Books Ltd., 1968.

HOLBROOK, JOHN and PRITCHARD, TERRY, *Control of a Business.* Business Publications Ltd., 1964.

WALLEY, B. H., *How to Make and Control a Profit Plan.* Business Books Ltd., 1969.

LOWE, C. H., *Critical Path Analysis by Bar Chart.* Business Publications Ltd., 1966.

WOODGATE, H. S., *Planning by Network.* Business Publications Ltd., 1967.

PILDITCH, JAMES and SCOTT, DOUGLAS, *The Business of Product Design.* Business Publications Ltd., 1965.

MORLEY, JOHN, *Launching a New Product.* Business Books Ltd., 1968.

CAIN, W. D., *Engineering Product Design.* Business Books Ltd., 1969.

CARSBERG, B. V. and EDEY, H. C., *Modern Financial Management.* Penguin modern management readings, 1969.

248

MORONEY, M. J., *Facts from Figures*. Pelican, 1956.

HOLLINGDALE, S. H. and TOOTILL, G. C., *Electronic Computers*. Pelican, 1965.

HUITSON, ALAN and KEEN, JOAN, *Essentials of Quality Control*. Heinemann, 1965.

OUGHTON, *Value Analysis and Value Engineering*. Pitman. 1969.

Index

251

of profits, 230; management framework, 225–6; recognition of opportunities, 229–30; reliable and accurate information, 227; resources, 224–5, 229; techniques, 228

Project control, 124–39: changes and change control, 137–9; cost analysis and control, 128, 130–5; decision making; 134–7; financial and progress areas, 125, 127; identification of objectives, 125, 127–8; key levels, 125–6; progress reporting, 128, 129

Project co-ordination, 25–8

Project definition, 42–57

Project management, meaning of, 1–19: key techniques, 10–18; Managers, 1–8; progress measurement, 18–19; systems approach, 10, 18; vital factors in management, 9

Project Managers, 1–8: choice of, 32–8; co-ordination routes, 6–7; definition, 2–7; descriptions in advertisements, 4–5; function lines, 6–8; management's attitude to, 29–30; responsibilities, 33

Project organization, 60–82: definition of task, 61–2; initial organization, 60–1; resources, 62–73; timescale, 73–82

Project orientated management, 39–40

Project risks, 187–8

Quality, 14, 50, 83–94

Quality assurance, 83–8: bought-out sub-assembly parts, 85–6; bought-out sub-system items, 86–7; continuous audit, 87–8; house design and manufacture, 85; special subcontracted items, 87; work breakdown, 84, 85

Quality control, 89–94: factory tests, 93–4; site tests, 94; statistics, 90–3

Rate of return (RR) method of financial evaluation, 203

Reliability, 94–6: computers, 96; redundancy, 95–6; system reliability, 95

Resources, 12, 49–50, 62–73, 229; and PERT, 159–63; capital budgets, 71–2; finance, 62–7; interplay with timescale, 73–82; inventory, 224–5; manpower, 68–70; materials and equipment, 69–71; services and facilities, 73; space, 72–3

Restraints on trade, 236–7

Rio Tinto Zinc Corporation, 198; Hamersley Iron Ore Subsidiary, 238–9

Services and facilities, 73

Shareholders capital, 218–20: cost of equity, 219–20; ordinary shareholders, 219–20; preference shareholders, 218–29

Size of project, 34–5

Space resources, 72–3

Structure of project management, 38–41

Subcontractors, 142–53: computer projects, 151–3; control of subcontractors, see separate entry; decision to subcontract, 142; reasons for subcontracting, 144; selection, 142–3

Surface charts, 108

Sykes, Alan, 219

System reliability, 95

Systems approach, 10, 18

Systems concept, 46, 48–9

Task forces, 41

Taxation, 234–5

Time value of money, 205–6

Timescale, 13, 50, 73–82: and PERT, 157, 159, 161–3; interplay with resources, 76–82

Ultramar Quebec oil refinery, 235–6